ATE DUE

CREATIVE DEMOCRACY

CREATIVE DEMOCRACY

Systematic Conflict Resolution and Policymaking in a World of High Science and Technology

Tom R. Burns and Reinhard Ueberhorst

Foreword by Willy Brandt

 PRAEGER

New York
Westport, Connecticut
London

Library of Congress Cataloging-in-Publication Data

Burns, Tom R.
  Creative democracy : systematic conflict resolution and
policymaking in a world of high science and technology / Tom R.
Burns and Reinhard Ueberhorst.
    p. cm.
    Bibliography: p.
    Includes index.
    ISBN 0-275-92957-4 (alk. paper)
    1. Science and state. 2. Technology and state. 3. Science—
Political aspects. 4. Technology—Political aspects.
I. Ueberhorst, Reinhard. II. Title.
Q125.B948 1988
338.9'26—dc19   88-25292

Library of Congress Catalog Card Number: 88-25292
ISBN: 0-275-92957-4

First published in 1988

Praeger Publishers, One Madison Avenue, New York, NY 10010
A division of Greenwood Press, Inc.

Printed in the United States of America

The paper used in this book complies with the Permanent
Paper Standard issued by the National Information Standards
Organization (Z39.48—1984).

10 9 8 7 6 5 4 3 2 1

CONTENTS

FOREWORD

Human progress has led to the present state of development where we can no longer allow science and technology to follow their own course. Incredible dangers and risks confront us, not only in instances such as Schernobyl and Harrisburg, but in the widespread destruction of forests and in water pollution. Our natural environment as well as our work and living environments are influenced and shaped more extensively and profoundly than ever before in human history by new and often difficult to understand technologies and complex sociotechnical systems. 'Progress' has resulted in a situation where it does not in fact help to merely oppose the further development of science and technology. Destructive technologies cannot be overcome by simply trying to impose restraints, but only by developing and selecting constructive, alternative technologies.

In the debate on nuclear energy in recent years, it has become perfectly clear for most that values and interests enter into each and every technology project. This implies, therefore, that for each and every technology there are always alternatives. The still widespread assumption that technological developments proceed autonomously or that they are the exclusive concern of those specialists involved in them can, therefore, be recognized as an ideological maneuver.

Technology must be subjected to democratic control in every case in which it shapes, and substantially impacts on, work life, housing, nutrition, and the natural environment. Where else in a democratic society should responsible discussion and decisionmaking over the design of our daily lives take place if not in democratically elected bodies established for the formation of political will and decisionmaking?

One of our most serious problems at present is dealing with new technologies, in part because of the difficulty of translating the knowledge or insights suggested above into political practice. We have only just begun to transform into practice the demands for constructive dialogue among experts, citizens, and politicians. The future of democracy -- perhaps for human survival itself -- will depend to a great extent on whether or not we succeed in good time to organize such dialogue effectively and convincingly.

In a democracy, politics is the issue for all citizens, and the issue of politics is the moderate design of social life. For this, we require principles and procedures to realize democratic decisionmaking in pursuit of responsible technological innovations and developments.

This book of Burns and Ueberhorst -- in which scientific reflections and practical experience are integrated in a fertile way -- is a welcome and exciting contribution to the development of new forms of democratic dialogue. These are related specifically to issues of science and technology. Besides shedding light on the basic principles of democratic discourse, the book offers a proposal for organizing such discourse so as to deal with technlogical issues and future technological developments. One need not agree with everything said to recognize that in this work a very important first step has been taken in the right direction.

I hope that the book will be read by many concerned readers from both areas -- the area of science and that of politics -- in order that the prevailing prejudices among experts, citizens, and politicians will be reduced and that major barriers to effective democratic control over technology will be systematically overcome.

Willy Brandt
Bonn, West Germany

ACKNOWLEDGMENTS

We are grateful to Bo Andersson, Kevin Avruch, Tom Baumgartner, Brack Brown, Robert Clark, James Douglas, Tom Dietz, Helena Flam, Ulf Himmelstrand, Giandomenico Majone, Thomas Meyer, Hannu Nurmi, and Peter Wagner for their comments and suggestions on earlier drafts. We want especially to thank Kenneth Boulding and James Douglas, who provided written comments and suggestions, a number of which have been incorporated into the text. Of course, we remain solely reponsible for the arguments and formulations presented in the book.

We are particularly grateful to Reinier de Man, Erasmus University, for his collaboration in the research and formulation of chapters 2 and 3 and to Lars Bruzeliius, Uppsala University Computer Center, for his technical advice and assistance in preparing this manuscript.

COPYRIGHT
ACKNOWLEDGMENTS

1

INTRODUCTION:
THE GLOBAL CHALLENGE

We have inherited a language of political alle-
giance which no longer speaks for the needs we
have, not as citizens, but as members of a common species.... every part of the planet is under
the same threat of extinction. Yet -- and this is
the truth before which thinking about politics
has stalled -- the more evident our common
needs as a species become, the more brutal becomes the human insistence on the claims of
difference. The centripetal forces of need, labour
and science which are pulling us together as a
species are counter-balanced by centrifugal forces, the claims of tribe, race, class section, region
and nation, pulling us apart.

Michael Ignatieff, *The Needs of Strangers*

Many of the major problems confronting the world today appear intractable, although there is widespread agreement
that something should be done about them:

o The threat of nuclear war

o Tense relations between the developed nations
    of the North and the developing nations
    of the South

o Environmental destruction and resource depletion

o Technological revolutions and their negative
    social and environmental impacts

o Continuing economic uncertainty

o Mass unemployment, especially among youth

Numerous proposals have been advanced to tackle these
problems. A basic difficulty is the lack of consensus about
what steps can and should be taken.

The two of us, a social scientist and a policy consultant
with professional political experience, have discussed and
argued at great length about some of the problems mentioned
above. We have been especially concerned about problems of
technology and the environment. Our concerns resulted in
this book. Related questions and issues which we took up
concern *the forms and quality of exchange among experts,
politicians, and citizens in a democratic society.* Modern
Western societies have undergone, and continue to undergo,
radical technical and social changes at ever-increasing rates.
Contemporary democracies are in large part unable to deal
with such changes. In our view, the democracies should be
redesigned in the face of these transformations.

The challenge, as we came to understand it, is to formulate innovative concepts and strategies for *democratic
practice.* First, these should lead to the development of new
democratic forms suitable for contemporary problems and issues. At the same time, they should be consistent with the
organizing principles and practices underlying conventional
democratic institutions. Secondly, they should enable politicians and citizens engaged in public deliberations to consult
and collaborate with technical and scientific experts in ways
that assure the integrity of systematic knowledge and the
pre-eminence of democratic politics.

This book examines the potential role of the social sciences in policy-making and contemporary politics, pointing out that there are serious barriers to communications between social scientists and policymakers. We have personally experienced these difficulties in our own conversations (also see Etzioni, 1985). Some of our more critical discussions ultimately took the form of an imaginary confrontation between a politician and a scholar, the latter a social scientist engaged or interested in policy research.

The scholar judges politicians to be hopelessly passive and unimaginative in the face of issues such as pollution and ecological crisis, arms development, and the risk of nuclear war, which threaten life as we know it, even survival itself.

To our scholar, most politicans are frivolous, preoccupied in the face of momentous issues with furthering their own personal ambitions, gaining institutional and financial support, or simply counting votes. The scholar argues, "Most contemporary politicians engage in symbolic gestures rather than in genuine efforts to address -- much less try to solve -- major contemporary problems. Their ignorance about modern technological developments and the driving forces underlying them, not least about weapon systems, is particularly appalling. They seem genuinely incapable of steering us toward anything better.

"Politicians fail to grasp what grave, possibly catastrophic miscalculations and oversights they commit while engaging in silly political games and 'Hollywood politics' for the benefit of the mass media. Often serious life-and-death matters are at stake. Even in instances where there is a genuine readiness to try to do something, their ignorance and lack of skill assure that little will happen or be accomplished."

Worst of all, at least in the scholar's eyes, is the lack of reflection among politicians about what they are doing -- or failing to do. Especially serious is their failure to realize the need to develop new political forms as well as strategies with which to tackle fundamental issues and problems facing humanity today. The forms and strategies of the past are in large part inadequate. All in all, the scholar considers politicians either incapable or unwilling to articulate original proposals and innovative strategies that would enable nations and their leaders to address major contemporary issues, above all those threatening survival itself.

Our politician retorts with a commentary on social scientists hunkering in their ivory towers, hopelessly narrow and irrelevant, precisely when it comes to important contemporary issues and the complexities of practical problemsolving. The vast sums of monies invested in social and policy research have failed to produce substantial results: nonobvious findings that would be useful or meaningful to political actors. The politician adds, "There aren't more than a handful of my colleagues who would read anything you or your social scientist colleagues wrote. Many politicians and others in practical affairs expected more of the social sciences. A good many are disillusioned and would drastically reduce research support unless social scientists can demonstrate the ability or the imagination to come up with new, useful concepts and methodologies.'

"You social scientists live in a world of modern cloisters, participating in rituals of reading, writing, and communion -- neither making the world nor even understanding it. You mix up right-wing or left-wing messages in your articles and books. I think that many of you wanted to be writers, but couldn't write or had nothing better to do than to become social scientists. You overproduce papers and books on irrelevant or esoteric subjects and problems.

"We politicians," our politician stresses, "are proud when we refer to our activities as nonacademic, as practical affairs. On the other hand, much of what you and your colleagues purport to be applied or practical social science knowledge concentrates on what was or is; little or nothing concerns what is possible and how it could be achieved.

"Many of you academicians say you want democracy. I realize that you don't necessarily mean by this that I have to follow 'the will of the people' when this conflicts with scientific evidence or systematic knowledge. At the very minimum, however, it must mean that a politician is constrained within limits set by the will and understanding of the people, or by the extent to which persuasion can change their viewpoints. Yet, whenever I try to operate within the democratic system, you say that I am engaging in silly political games and Hollywood politics for the benefit of the mass media. Where the will of the people coincides with the findings of science -- and you must allow me to know the will of the people better than you do as this is my business and not yours -- social science is not telling me anything I don't already know. Where science conflicts with the will or understanding of the people -- and there are many examples of this, not least in economics and in technological areas -- then in a democracy, the rules are geared to ensure that science comes out second best.

"You cannot have democracy without politics because democracy is a system in which we politicians acquire the power to make political decisions by competing for the people's votes. I do my best to influence those votes in what I think is the socially right as well as scientifically correct way. But if the voters prefer the socially wrong or scientifically incorrect way, the politician who shares their preference -- and not I -- will acquire the power to make the decision."

Obviously, our imaginary representatives, the scholar and the politician, embody the contrasting perspectives of their respective professions. They have very different ways of thinking, arguing, and making judgments. Of course, our politician may be one of the rare politicians deeply concerned about and involved in questions of science and technology. He may try to understand and to adapt himself to the tribal customs and forms of discourse of scientific communities. And the scholar might be one of those social scientists who attempts to imagine how a politician thinks and acts and how this can be related, if at all, to scientific method and knowledge. Somehow they might find common ground to begin effective dialogue and creative collaboration, but this is fraught with difficulties.

Our scholar and politician are, of course, stereotypes, but stereotypes reflecting a definite reality. It is precisely this reality, that, in our view, must be systematically addressed if democracy in a world of high science and technology is to be sustained and developed.

In our view, social scientists and politicians give far too little attention to processes of communication between different viewpoints, interests, and expertise. In part, this is because, on the one hand, many social scientists have a conception of "neutral science," making it difficult for them to engage themselves or to define appropriate roles for themselves in policy-making and contemporary politics. On the other hand, politicians are often simply content to use, whenever possible, expert groups including social scientists to develop their strategies and to strengthen the machinery of political influence and acceptance. Yet, as we argue later, both mutual isolation as well as many forms of collusion between scientists and politicians undermine democratic decisionmaking and result in undesirable, even catastrophic outcomes.

Some politicians and some scientists sense this problem -- and speak out about it -- but they cannot change it without establishing new forms of interaction between politics and science (Majone, 1986; Ueberhorst, 1986).

This became our collective challenge. It led to the formulations in this book. Both of us feel that without new concepts and strategies of conflict resolution and policy-making, humanity has no long-term future. It will destroy itself -- suddenly, unequivocally, in nuclear holocaust, or gradually, by destroying its resource base and polluting the environment to a point beyond which the present human race cannot be sustained. Many of our present-day institutional arrangements, "rules of the game", and dominant political styles are inappropriate or counterproductive in dealing with such problems as technological revolution, ecological catastrophe, and the arms race.

Given this depressing state of affairs, we agreed, from our different perspectives and professional orientations, to devote ourselves to exploring and developing new concepts and strategies to tackle major contemporary problems, especially those relating to technological development.

Of course, there are those who will say nothing can be done; earlier attempts have failed. Technological development proceeds relentlessly, autonomously. It cannot be stopped or steered. In the area of disarmament and world peace, they point out, "The Soviet government wants permanent revolution and the United States persistently strives for advantage in military technology. There can be no settlement.

In our view, we have no viable option other than to engage each other -- and as many others as possible -- in the task of searching for and developing new concepts, methods, and strategies with which to tackle critical contemporary problems and conflicts. In a certain sense, we agree with Sinai's (1978:211) characterization of the crisis of democracy (but stressing at the same time that the undemocratic nations of the world also suffer, probably more so, from a lack of adequate knowledge and collective capability in the face of the challenges of future survival):

> The democratic governments of the West are everywhere in decline. They lack the intellectual capacities to master the complexities which have emerged as a result of heedless economic growth and chaotic political development. Authority lacks confidence and the people lack confidence in authority. The demands on democratic government for leadership and management have grown immensely while the capacities of democratic government have everywhere disastrously shrivelled. Image-making replaces policy. Everywhere powerful sectional economic and political interests subvert any coherent view of the public

interest. Dominated by powerful economic interests (and power-hungry expert), swayed by mass tastes and standards, torn by exhausting and murderous factional conflicts, our democratic states suffer from a breakdown of community, a loss of all sense of civic obligation and cooperation and a universal pursuit of self-interest.

In the following chapter, we discuss technology and science in their societal context. The chapter is written primarily to provide a simplified but basic understanding of the nature of science and technology. We argue that relatively few people are involved in deciding about and shaping major sociotechnical developments such as nuclear energy systems, telecommunications, genetic engineering, and "star wars" preparations, with their substantial impacts on work and employment, culture, security, and survival itself. Technological innovation and development under these conditions are not only incompatible with elementary principles of democracy. They are highly risk-filled, since important human values and life-forms are typically ignored in a relatively closed process of technological design and development.

Chapter 3 tries to clarify the uneasy, sometimes very difficult relationship between scientific expertise and politics (Bulmer, 1987). We argue that the separation of science and politics, even if it would be desirable, is not feasible in the modern world. An informed politics requires science and other systematic knowledge. But the producers of systematic knowledge, in their involvement in policy-making, risk becoming ideologues or pawns subject to the political rules of the game. They are freer to act outside of the normative framework and methodology governing the scientific production of systematic knowledge, nonetheless claiming the halo of science.

Chapters 2 and 3 together suggest serious threats to two major institutions in modern society: democracy and science. On the one hand, democracy is threatened with becoming irrelevant. Its institutions formally ignore or passively acquiesce in major sociotechnical decisions reached elsewhere. These very decisions have, or are likly to have, powerful and often unforeseeable impacts on the social and natural environments. The general public and its political representatives lack the cognitive frame or the institutional support to ask relevant or essential questions or to play "devil's advocate."

On the other hand, scientific and other expertise applied to policy-making is all too often subverted or misused. Indeed, scientific enterprise plays an apparently paradoxical role in the development of modern society. It contributes to sociotechnical revolutions that, at a fundamental level, are led and shaped by relatively few persons. At the same time, science and systematic expertise are often mobilized and used in policy-making to provide legitimacy and to assure "democratic acceptance" of particular policies or definitions of reality. Potential opposition to policy decisions and technological developments may be disarmed by the authority of science.

Chapters 4 and 5 address questions such as the following:

What kind of science and expertise does democratic politics require in order to realize its spirit? In what ways can democratic steering and consensus formation be organized and carried out in a world of experts, where the principle of technocracy tends to prevail?

Similarly, what kind of politics does science and modern experise require in order to contribute to informed and reliable decisions -- decisions likely to be judged later as sensible -- in shaping human futures in intelligent and reasonably ways?

Such questions provide a point of departure for us to propose new strategies to increase public awareness of, and democratic control over, major technological developments and, ultimately, human futures. We stress the importance of discussion and consensus formation to democracy, (in part correcting what we consider to be excessive stress placed on 'voting' and 'majority rule').

In the model of what we refer to as "organized democratic discourse," political groups, organizations, or parties formulate or reconstruct alternative sociotechnical futures, or *systemic alternatives*. These entail different approaches or strategies to tackle the problems or goals with which a proposed technology or sociotechnical system is designed to deal. Examples of such sociotechnical alternatives are: nuclear versus non-nuclear energy systems, private car transportation as opposed to public transportation systems (or various mixed systems), private versus public health care systems, alternative systems for utilizing computers and information technologies in factories and offices, and alternative defense systems.

Scientists and other technical experts play an important role in assisting those in the political arena *to formulate and articulate their systemic alternatives,* specifying ways in which such options might be established, organized, financed, and operated.

The alternatives that are formulated, examined and, compared should be presented in ways the participants holding different perspectives can accept. The advocates of each systemic alternative should have access to expertise that they trust either as being genuinely neutral and professional or as being loyal to their option. The conceptualization of systemic alternatives suggested or formulated by political actors feed into processes of discourse, reformulation, and negotiation among the agents.

Apel (1979:83-84), drawing on Habermas, has made similar suggestions:

> (O)ur present post-industrial planetary civilisation, for the first time in history, forces us to live together in the same boat ... argumentative dis-

course ... provides the only possibility for rescu-
ing and protecting as much as possible of the
richness of personal and socio-cultural individu-
alities. Precisely this is testified to *by the numerous international conferences about every vital
problem of humanity which we are informed
about through the mass media almost every day.*
it is philosophically interesting, I suggest, that
all these conferences today take the form of ar-
gumentative discourse. Their participants, not-
withstanding their strong strategic purposes or,
respectively, provisos, must at least *feign* the intention of solving the problems raised by conflicts on the basis of intersubjectively valid arguments in the above sense. Even if there should be
argumentatively irreconcilable conflicts due to
incommensurable forms of life,... we have to
face the urgent task of providing a basis for co-
existence, or mutual tolerance, by coming to
consensus about more fundamental opinions,
interests, or purposes. Thus, mutual tolerance
and striving for consensus are *not* in contra-
diction with each other, and the ideal of an indefinite communication-community is *not*
equivalent to the ideal of illiberal collectivism.

Many new forms of organized democratic discourse
and "negotiation," in elementary versions, have already
emerged and are being utilized, as Apel points out. We consider this book a constructive attempt to increase awareness
of, and to systematize knowledge about, these forms of creative democracy. We explore institutional innovations necessary to facilitate the emergence and development in a
modern democracy of creative discourse and constructive negotiation relating to issues of high science and technology.
We propose a way for experts and nonexperts to work together to explore and develop technical alternatives and, in

doing so, to participate in a social learning process that will enable them to better understand the implicit assumptions and underlying values in technical models and proposals and their possible consequences if carried out in practice.

Our proposal entails a democratic strategy to facilitate conflict resolution and policy-making relating to major technological issues and developments in modern society. The proposed strategy differs substantially from bureaucratic, technocratic, and coercive strategies. The bureacratic strategy is one in which diversity of opinion and potential conflict are to a great extent ignored and a few agents -- largely outside public scrutiny -- make strategic decisions concerning technological developments. This is at the expense of, or risk to, the citizenry -- including also future generations of citizens. The democratic strategy differs as well from coercive strategies that utilize the police powers of the modern state to suppress public diversity of opinion concerning technological issues and to impose sociotechnical systems on civil society, such as nuclear power plants and systems of telecommunications.

Systematic democratic discourse, in our view, has the potential not only to realize basic human rights but also to effectively address and deal with major contemporary problems relating to choice among possible alternative sociotechnical futures.

2

TECHNOLOGY AND SOCIETY

The Church welcomes technological progress and receives it with love, for it is an indubitable fact that technological progress comes from God and must lead to him.

Pope Pius XII (1876-1958), Christmas Message, 1953

We are well aware ... that the future of man and mankind is threatened, radically threatened, despite very noble intentions, by men of science. And it is menaced because the tremendous results of their discoveries, especially regarding the natural sciences, have been and continue to be exploited -- for ends which have nothing to do with the prerequisites of science, but with the ends of destruction and death.

Pope John Paul II, Speech before UNESCO, June 2, 1980.

Both quotations from Coppock (1984)

2.1   INTRODUCTION

Many technological developments threaten to undermine important social values and practices, at the same time that they improve production or the quality of goods and services, reduce costs, or provide other advantages and benefits that motivated their introduction and development. For instance, the growing use of computers and information technologies not only enables human beings to do things they were unable to do before, but also changes work conditions and power relationships in society, provides a basis for more effective state monitoring and policing of citizens, and plays an increasingly important role in the development of modern weapon systems[1].

In spite of a few "voices in the wilderness," political awareness and discourse about the implications of the information revolution and about major developments in biotechnology, genetic engineering, and other contemporary technology developments have been minimal. There is little or no systematic consideration of *possible alternative developments.* In general, such matters rarely became political issues in Western countries.

There tends to be a great gap between individual everyday experiences and awareness, on the one hand, and global social and physical-environmental consequences, on the other. The latter are in many instances indirect and extended into very distant and complex futures. Typically, political leaders and common citizens grasp only vaguely at best the relationship between, for instance, information technologies or new genetic techniques and basic values, such as "sense of security," "political rights and freedom," "cultural and personal integrity," among others.

This failure has often allowed the formation of new sociotechnical systems and related technical and social changes that compromised or undermined the core values of societies. Many developments take place without a serious and systematic assessment of potentially negative consequences. In our view, the values of improved production, cost savings, engineering and managerial development, and "economic progress" (all of which might be realized through technological development) should be weighted more systematically against potential losses, particularly important "soft" or less obvious and long-term social values, such as "sense of personal and social security" and "quality of life."

In many instances, harmful developments can be avoided, provided citizens and politicians are sufficiently aware of what is at stake and can translate awareness into political action. This increases the likelihood that technologies and sociotechnical systems are designed from the beginning or carefully regulated -- before they wreak large-scale havoc. Of course, no guarantee is possible; the future is far too uncertain.

In this chapter we shall examine factors in technological development and, in particular, the relationship between technological development and societal power. Major sociotechnical developments today reflect a substantial concentration of power to shape and influence the future. Democracy tends to be subordinated to technocracy. While our treatment is necessarily brief, it is detailed enough, we hope, to provide a basis on which to understand the nature of technology and to suggest new relationships between politics, technical knowledge, and social power.

2.2   TECHNOLOGY AND SOCIETY

The production and use of tools and technical aids is found in all spheres of human activity and in all historical periods. What differs today from several thousand or even a hundred years ago are the scale and organization of complex tool use, the rapidity with which new tools are developed and put into use, and the scope and intensity with which innovations in tools impact on and transform social life and the physical environment.

Lindblom (1977:30) points out that the essential feature of the technological revolutions launched in Western civilization was in putting two resources to work on a scale never before attempted: machines of great variety, made possible by accelerated science and engineering; and coal (and later oil and nuclear energy) as a source of power to run them. He adds, "Just as the organization of the mines called for organized business enterprises, so also did the man-machine coordination necessary to take advantage of the productive potential of the new machines."

The broad concept of "industrial revolution" fails to encompass the variety and scope of technological and organizational revolutions which have shaped modern society, and continue to shape it at ever-increasing rates. These are, among others:

- New techniques of metallurgy and machine-making; the widespread use of machines in economic production (the technological revolution proper).

- Great developments of energy, the consequences and side effects of which are not yet completely under control or even fully known. Nuclear energy is the most publicized example, but earlier revolutions in the use of fossil fuels (coal, gas, oil) increased energy resource use many times over and had impacts about which we are still making discoveries (atmospheric carbon dioxide pollution, acid rain, among others).

- The revolution in communications: ships, railroads, automobiles, air travel, telephone, telegraph, satellites and other forms of tele-communication. Transportation speeds have increased by a factor of about 1000 between 1928 and 1980: from 180 (about 112 miles) per hour to the speed of satellites that are now almost routinely sent into orbit.

- Great developments in chemistry. We live in a world of plastic materials, artificial fibers, antibiotics, and pharmaceuticals, most of which did not exist or only existed in minute quantities at the turn of the century.

- Writing (and eventually the printing press) and the clock are other essential innovations: writing and the printing press for their role in recording, accumulating, and codifying knowledge and regulations and in revolutionalizing communication among human groups; the clock for providing the technological basis for precise timing and coordination among large numbers of people and activities, even those located in different solar-time regions.

- The revolution in social organization and administration (especially the development of means to extend them to control over national and international areas). This would not have been possible without transformations in communications[2].

- The revolutions in education, research, and in general, the social production and dissemination of systematic knowledge and its applications.

Some of the transformations mentioned above are called new not because they have never before taken place anywhere but because but because now they are being extended worldwide and at a much faster pace than previously

(Deutsch, 1980:130). Deutsch (130) notes: "They are therefore of a different quality. In this connection, the social trasformation is greater than each individual discovery or invention that we know." Deutsch suggests that in order to find parallels for the technological breakthroughs and transformations, one has to think in terms of the thousands and millions of years of biological evolution.

These technological developments, successfully organized and administered in sociotechnical systems, have brought immense improvements in productivity and in the wealth of many nations. Conditions of human life have been, and continue to be, transformed (Rosenberg, 1982:246)[3]. One should stress the qualitative aspects of the revolution as much as the quantitative, economic ones. Human beings have been incorporated into complex sociotechnical systems designed and managed by others. Moreover, the major tools of modern production, including the know-how and resources to produce and develop new tools and techniques, are concentrated in the hands of relatively few agents, such as top managers and the engineering staff of large-scale, often transnational corporations (Galbraith's "technostructure").

The social scientific study of technology focuses our attention on major forces shaping and reshaping todayés people and society. Rosenberg argues (1982:39):

> Technology is what mediates between man and his relationship with the external, material world. But in acting upon that material world, man not only transforms it for his own useful purposes (that is to say, Nature becomes one of the organs of his activity) but he also, unavoidably, engages in an act of self-transformation and self-realization. "By thus acting on the external world and changing it, he at the same time changes his own nature" (Karl Marx). Technology, therefore, is at the center of those activities that are distinctively human.

But what is technology[4]? Unfortunately, one cannot find simple, clear answers to this question in the scientific and engineering communities. Indeed, there is considerable conceptual and analtyical confusion about such terms as technology, technique, tools, technical systems. "Technology" in particular may refer, among other things, to (a) objects or artifacts themselves, (b) knowledge or know-how about producing or using the artifacts, and (c) the entire system of artifacts, knowledge, and organizationaland institutional arrangements surrounding the production and use of artifacts (Bereano, 1976; Hummon, 1984; McGinn, 1978; Margolis, 1978; Rosenberg, 1982; Schon, 1969; Mitcham, 1978; Weingart, 1974).

Below we suggest some basic terminology, making distinctions and formulating concepts with which to understand the social -- and political -- nature of technology. These will prove useful in our later discussions.

Technologies are physical tools of action, extending human powers. Technologies as artifacts (tools, machinery, equipment, buildings, etc.) extend the capabilities of human action and are, therefore, sources of power (Schon,1969; Hummon, 1984; Margolis, 1978; McGinn, 1978). The artifacts of technology are often used to achieve certain objectives or to solve certain problems, where improvement in performance (speed, quality, reliability, etc.) can be ascertained. Artefacts are also utilized as objects of worship and symbols, that is, where instrumentality is not readily apparent (Mitcham, 1978).[5])

Technology control and use are governed by social rule systems. Technologies as physical artifacts are, of course, subject to the laws of nature. At the same time, human agents make up social rules about their use: who controls the technology, and its uses and benefits (or pays compensation for some of its impacts); who uses it under specified circumstances; how it is to be used; for what purposes; under what conditions; where and when (Burns and Flam, 1987). Technology from this perspective should be examined in relation to the fabric of everyday actions and interactions in which human actors participate and from which they derive meaning (Winner, 1983:258). As Winner suggests (262):

> A deceptive quality of technical objects and processes -- their promiscuous utility, the fact that they can be "used" in this way or in that -- blinds us to the ways in which they structure what we are able to do and the ways in which they settle important issues *de facto* without appearing to do so. Thus, for example, the freedom we enjoy in the realm of "use" is mirrored in our extreme dependency upon vast, centralized, complicated, remote and increasingly vulnerable artificial systems.

Technologies are instruments of social action with consequences. The introduction of new technologies and the development of technological systems entail more than setting up and using new machines and other physical artifacts. It entails social re-organizing and the making of new rules[6] as well as the adaptation, transformation or replacement of old ones. Effective use -- or even any "suitable use" of the technology -- requires in most cases some minimal knowledge and utilization of operative rules. Indeed, the design of the technology presupposes knowledgeable, competent users -- that is, human agents who have or can acquire the necessary competence within an acceptable time frame[7]. The design presupposes, in particular, that users or potential users know or can learn essential operational information about the technology, its performance characteristics, strong and weak features, and so forth. They should also possess certain values concerning treatment of the technology, its utilization, and its maintenance. Finally, users must learn specific rules and procedures of operation, maintenance, and repair. Of course, some technologies, such as those intended for mass consumption, are designed so that minimum knowledge is required in order to use them effectively. The "grammar of use" may be no more than a few rules about which buttons to push, when to push them, and precisely how to do so.

Some technological areas, such as pharmaceuticals and building construction, have long been governed by elaborate laws and regulations. Professional groups (for example, pharmacists or architects) may mobilize to establish or maintain a monopoly of technology control in their area of competence and production (drugs and building design, respectively). Their strategy may be to establish policies or laws aimed at preventing the introduction of certain innovations or obtaining monopoly control over them. Even well-established areas periodically undergo dramatic technological changes. Entirely new technologies and production techniques enter the field. Our later examples point up some of the social and political games that take place in connection with technological innovation and development, a subject to which we shall return later in the book.

The social organization of technology suggests the concept of sociotechnical system. Social activities involving technology are organized and, to a greater or lesser extent, institutionalized in complex sociotechnical systems, for example, a nuclear power plant, organ transplant systems, or telecommunication systems. Knowledge of technology-in-use presupposes knowledge of social organization and, in particular, knowledge of the organizing principles and rules of human institutions.

The concept of a sociotechnical system is particularly useful, even essential, when one considers complex, large-scale technologies such as factory systems, nuclear power plants, electrificiation systems, and transportation systems, among others. Such systems consist, on the one hand, of complex technical and physical structures that are designed to produce or transform certain things and, on the other, of social institutions and legal orders designed to structure and regulate the activities of the human beings involved. The technostructures may be owned or managed by different agents. The knowledge of these different structures may be dispersed among different occupations and professions. Thus, a variety of groups, social networks, and organizations may be involved in the construction, operation and maintenance of distinct technostructures. The problem of establishing and mantaining a sociotechnical system becomes one of *linking together different social and physical structures into a* more or less integrated, operative or functioning *whole.* For example, electric systems consist of hydropower facilities, coal-fired electric generators, nuclear power plants, distribution nets, and a wide spectrum of different end users and end uses. Organizing and managing such systems is a formidable design and management challenge, but one which engineers and managers have shown extraordinary inventiveness and skill in tackling.

The social organizational aspects of technology in social action have been stressed by Rosenberg (1982:247-8): "(T)echnologies are more than bits of dissembodied hardware. They function within societies where their usefulness is dependent upon managerial skills, upon organizational structures and upon the operation of incentive systems."

Technologies, including massive physical structures such as buildings and dams, entail the application of organizing principles and rules governing the control and use of the technology. Technological innovations evoke opportunities and pressures to change established principles and rules. But since organizations and societies vary in their institutional and socio-cultural make-up, the context of innovation varies, and therefore, the types of opportunities, challenges, and social tensions generated in connection with technological innovation vary. This suggests that innovations in organizing principles and rules formulated or developed in connection with the introduction and use of a new technology may not always "fit in", or may not be compatible with, existing social and physical structures.

Incompatibilities between a new technology and conventional sociotechnical systems hinder the introduction of new technologies, unless the incompatible elements are overcome by "change agents" and "entrepreneurs." The latter mobilize resources and exercise social power (Baumgartner and Burns, 1984; Burns, 1985). In this way new sociotechnical systems, such as an automated factory or a fast-breeder reactor, are established or old ones are transformed. Such restructuring will not take place if the social agents motivated to introduce and develop a new technology cannot mobilize the necessary social power and other resources (capital, expertise, infrastructure, legal rights, political support, etc.).

Some technological innovations or sociotechnical developments require rule changes in the spheres of, for instance, production, finance, administration, politics, education and science. The success of a new technology or sociotechnical development will depend on whether entrepreneurs and change agents in the different areas can form alliances or networks across spheres in order to bring about rule changes in multiple spheres as well as inter-sphere rule changes. In the absence of sufficiently powerful change agents or networks, the technological innovation will be aborted or seriously delayed. Some impediments arise as collective expressions of vested interests and "critical assessments" on the part of groups who successfully mobilize in order to block undesirable technological developments, such as nuclear power.

The history of the development of sociotechnical systems, such as the assembly-line factory as well as hydropower, electrification, and nuclear systems, point up that the organizational and political problems are as much a challenge -- and an area of great innovation -- as the purely technical. Laudan (1984:91) stresses this point: "Entrepreneurs need technical skills, but in order to design systems on this scale (electrical systems, etc.) they have to employ many other skills as well, economic, social, and political."

The problems of control, organization, and management in the extension of human action through the use of tools has entailed *qualitative shifts -- and new orders of magnitude --* in going from hammer, knife, hut, and fire to modern machines, buildings, and nuclear power plants. The modern organization of major sociotechnical systems -- whether in capitalist societies or communist societies -- has entailed *the separation of most participants from the processes of design, organization, management, and control of these systems.* Such processes are in the hands of relatively small elite groups. Designers and producers shape and develop such systems, but typically not consistently, according to their perceptions of the needs or demands of users and potential users. Their own interests and organizing principles also play a role, of course.

2.3   TECHNOLOGY AND SCIENCE

The link between science and technology is a complex one. Some researchers see it as a close, hierarchical relationship: science is the basis of technology; technology is applied science (e.g., Bunge, 1981). Others see the relationship as one of mutual interdependence (e.g., Rosenberg in some of his writings) or of integration. Häfele (1963) refers to "project science" such as sending a rocket to the moon, developing breeder and fusion reactors or other high-level science-input technology systems. Still others see it as a very loose connection, with technology and technological development enjoying in many areas a high degree of autonomy from science (Burns and Flam, 1987; Rosenberg, 1982).

The discussion here will be necessarily brief but it outlines our basic theses.

1. Science is one of several bases of technology. Much more knowledge than that of science alone goes into the creation and development of technology. Of course, the scientific content of technology varies from case to case. Obviously, the scientific input into such technologies as nuclear power and bio-technology is extremely high, whereas it is considerably lower and less necessary in the production of wood products, clothes, and simple machine tools. At the same time, as Rosenberg (1982) and others have argued, technological innovations and developments have, in many instances, stimulated and even made basic contributions to scientific knowledge, as the case of the steam engine points up.

2. Technology entails non-scientific elements because of its integration into human action and social organization, for instance, production and consumption activities. It is fitted into practical, cognitive, material, and institutional structures. *Therefore, it contains types of knowledge which are entirely social, political, and cultural.* Basic science has a more purely "cognitive character," entailing knowing rather than doing (Layton, 1972). *Its "truths" need not necessarily be fitted into the social world as it is organized and functions.*

3. In general, there are differences in aims, methods, and bases of legitimacy in science and technology. In a word, they represent different social forms of activity. McGinn (1978:195-6), referring to Nietzsche, writes:

> For Nietzsche, science, a different form of human activity, constitutes an essentially Socratic optimistic and would-be triumphant approach to dealing with the problematic nature of the human condition, as opposed to, say, the consolatory approach implicit in the tragic world view. Science, Nietzsche claims, places something akin to an absolute value on truth and assumes that

life can be made meaningful by understanding it through rational, intellectual means.

As a different way of appropriating the world, technology, with its animating Promethean Geist, is also optimistic and assigns a kind of categorical value to "technological progress." The predominant spirit informing post-Renaissance technological activity, a spirit liberally fueled by its remarkable successes, assumes that, ceteris paribus, the human condition can only be ameliorated and rendered more meaningful by ongoing technological progress (i.e. improvements in the knowledge or resource or methodological sectors of various technologies).

The belief that there is a rational solution to human problems reflects the concept of reality which science and technology share. However, science entails the systematic development of descriptive rules and principles, including scientific generalizations and "laws," and the procedures to formulate, test, and elaborate such rules. Technology, in contrast, consists of a rule framework stressing *knowledge of the world that can be used in human action, in producing or doing something and, in this sense, is eminently practical.* Weingart (1984:121) emphasizes this point:

> The properties of technology which it shares with action in the concrete world is its uniqueness; the "diversity of practical conditions" (context dependence) requires "unique methods," namely experiments on machines at real scale and under realistic conditions.

Technology is not simply "applied science" but much more[8].

Although science and technological knowledge, considered on an abstract general level, can be thought of as generated by a common process of rational problem-solving, they differ in fundamental ways as forms of knowledge and as social forms (Laudan, 1984:10). Technology, in contrast to science, is a part of sociotechnical systems with concrete activities and social organization that have a direct impact on people's lives. People rarely react to scientific developments in the ways they react only rarely to technological developments. Political assessments of and reactions to "scientific ideas" or results do occur in the modern world, as the contemporary histories of fascism, communism, and religious fundamentalism demonstrate. These reactions occur *largely on ideological grounds.* Science and its theories come into conflict with the views of religion and ideology about nature, humanity, and society, but *do not have direct, concrete impacts on social life, people's conditions, and their concrete relation to nature and to one another, in short, on power relations.* On the one hand, a substantial part of science is "autonomous" in this sense[9]. On the other hand, technology and technological development have a practical, direct impact, and may sometimes, as in the case of nuclear power facilities, evoke concrete socio-political struggles, that decide the short- to medium-term fate of the technology.

2.4 TECHNOLOGY AND SOCIAL POWER: THE CASE OF INFORMATION TECHNOLOGIES

As suggested earlier, there exist *cultural and institutional infrastructures* around technologies and technology-action complexes. Technological development entails transformations of these infrastructures. In order that a new technology be used effectively -- to accomplish those things that it has been designed to do -- certain cultural and institutional changes are required. These may be difficult to bring about, both because of political opposition and because of high uncertainty associated with any radical restructuring. Mismatches or incompatibility between technology design and social infrastructure explain in part why technology transfer to Third World countries from the First World so often fails (Baumgartner et al., 1986).

Even in developed countries, we see many instances of mismatches between new technologies and the sociotechnical systems into which they are introduced. There may be political struggles associated with such mismatches[10]. Those actors (such as engineers and managers) who wish to introduce and make more efficient use of the technology push for changes in the organization of production, occupational structures, and production norms. Employees, labor unions, professions/occupations, and political agents with vested interests or values in the established structures -- or who are opposed to the utilization of or the risks involved in introducing new technologies -- resist those efforts. Much of the opposition to the introduction and development of technology -- for example, on the part of labor unions in the past and "green movements" today -- has been treated as anti-modern and irrational, even if it was grounded rationally in commitments to core cultural values and institutional forms.

That these struggles may result in radically different outcomes from those anticipated is wellknown from comparisons of the outcomes of the introduction of new technologies in diverse countries, or in different sectors of the same country, some, for example, with traditional and others with innovation-oriented managements and labor forces. Variations in outcomes also are found between companies in the same industry.

The point is that, on the one hand, the introduction and development of new technologies entail changing established organizing principles and rules. On the other hand, those with vested interests in, or value commitments to, these systems may struggle to maintain them. The structuring and restructuring of sociotechnical systems have impacts, sometimes of a radical nature, on everyday actions and interactions. In this regard, Winner (1983:251, 254) stresses:

> Technologies are templates which influence the shape and texture of political life. Thus, the construction of any technical system that involves human beings as operating parts amounts to a partial reconstruction of social roles and relationships. Similarly, the very act of using the kinds of machines, technologies and systems available to us generates patterns of activities and expectations that soon become "second nature" to us. We do indeed "use" telephones, automobiles, and electric lights in the conventional sense of picking them up and putting them down. But our world soon becomes one in which telephony, automobility, and electric lighting are forms of life in the sense that life would scarely be thinkable without them.... Yet if the experience of the past two centuries shows us anything, it is certainly that technologies are not only aides in human activity, but also powerful occasions for reshaping that activity. In no area of inquiry is this fact more important than in our own discipline, the study of politics.

By using technology in concrete and practical activities, actors acquire new experience; they learn and change. They revise their everyday situational analyses as well as their operative rules relating to the activities in which the technology is employed. Technology's dialectical interplay with human action gives occasion for the re-structuring and transformation of the rule systems making up institutional arrangements and the culture of society.

The fundamental decisions about the design, development, and introduction of technology are largely in the hands of relatively small elite groups (technical, economic, and socio-political). These influence, out of all proportion to their numbers, the lives of the vast majority through the impact of technological development on social life. Indeed, in some instances the survival of humankind, or at least life as we know it, is at stake.

This power is an abstract power to shape future social processes and social conditions, for instance, through nuclear power construction or the development and application of genetic engineering, powers in many ways much more formidable than that grounded on controlling traditional forms of violence or means of production.

This idea is pointed up by the contemporary revolutions in micro-electronics and communications. In particular, robotization and computerization promise, among other things, to transform within decades occupational structures and employment conditions as well as related educational and training systems; to intensify control over people's lives at work; to extend the bureaucratization of organizational life and social life generally; and to enhance the possibilities for central access to and control over vast amounts of information and social intelligence; and even to substantially alter free-time and leisure activities. Let us for the purposes of our discussion here concentrate only on transformations of occupational structures, work life, and employment conditions.

There are major disagreements about the long-term implications for work and employment of the micro-electronic revolution. The latter entails (1) automated production which combines computers, numerically-controlled machines, and robots in product design and manufacture; and (2) telematics, which combines computer information handling with telecommunications technology -- telephone, television, teleprinters, satellite transmission, among other technologies (Harris, 1986). Optomists and advocates (Daniel Bell, Alvin Toffler, John Naisbitts, Marilyn Ferguson, among others) stress the advantages and gains of the micro-electronic revolution: in productivity, cost savings, elimination of monotonous and physically wearing tasks, dramatic expansion of scarce productive capabilities in the form of robots and automation, opportunities for professional development, and opportunities for more humanitarian, self-managing work forms, among others.

The claim is made that the technological revolution will result in a net increase in jobs and that employees who lose their jobs due to robotization and computerization will to some degree, through retraining, be able to obtain new, better positions. Many of the new positions, it is argued, will themselves be created through technological development. Although many companies and occupations will suffer because of inferior technology, there will be for most a dramatic and positive transition to a new economic order.

Others (e.g., Colley, Markus, Ruskin, Choate) argue that the transformations and potential negative effects (economic, political, social) of the robotic and computer revolutions will far exceed those of the industrial revolution. Labor representatives, among others, complain about a number of adverse effects of the revolution, in particular large-scale unemployment in industrial areas and de-skilling of many of the remaining jobs. They stress that the work pace has accelerated and become more demanding, decision-making and human interaction have been systematically removed from many jobs, and, most importantly, computers have been increasingly used to monitor and control workers, all of which contribute to the dehumanization of many workplaces.

The critics argue that the creation of highly technical positions will not suitably employ workers displaced by the robotization of factories and the computerization of offices. In any case, there have been -- and will continue to be -- many losers in these transformations, namely, those in occupations, industries, and communities that are displaced by the revolution as well as those who have great difficulty in gaining access (Weinstein, 1983:2).

In a recent review, Draper(1985:46) argues that major parts of the industrial working class will disappear as a result of robotization, for instance, welders, painters, machinists and toolmakers, machine operators, inspectors, and industrial assemblers. He adds that there is no guarantee that the transformation will automatically create in the foreseeable future new jobs for the men and women it displaces . Estimates in the United States and England indicate substantial *net elimination* of jobs[11]. A Carnegie-Mellon study on automation and employment indicates that by the year 2025, robotic equipment will replace almost all operator jobs in U.S. manufacturing as well as a large number of routine jobs outside of the manufacturing sector (Hunt and Hunt, 1983; Harris, 1986).

This development may, over the longrun, be compatible to some extent with an aging population whose active participation in the labor force is also declining. In the short to medium run, however, the size of the work force will not decline, and new jobs in services are not likely to be created fast enough to absorb those workers made redundant by robotics. Furthermore, service jobs of comparable pay and skill to those lost in manufacturing are not likely to be created. Indeed, some fear the impact of office automation even more than they fear robotization of manufacturing (Draper, 1985:51); Leontief and Duchin (1985) suggest that 0.75 million managers and 5.0 million clerical workers in the United States may find themselves technologically unemployed by 1990. As Harris (1986:32) notes, the 1980s have seen the rapid introduction of automated equipment into the office, as organizations automate their payroll processing, inventory control, production scheduling, accounting, performance monitoring, printing, routine wordprocessing, and photocoping. Telematic equipment has begun to replace much of the traditional means of communication used in office work. He concludes that the office of the future will probably be an integrated electronic workstation where telematic and automated equipment will make possible the electronic processing of vast quantities of information in a fraction of the time now involved in processing the same quantity of information.

Concerning the transformation of industry -- and the conditions of employment in industry -- Draper (1985:46) argues: "If we pretend that this transformation will automatically create new jobs for the men and women it displaces, we will probably end up with a vastly expanded underclass, not a vastly expanded pool of computer programmers." Draper and others point out that *robotics is specifically designed to cut the need for labor. Moreover, it is not designed to deal with the formidable problems of finding jobs for industrial workers or training them for white-collar work.* Shaiken (1985) stresses that, unlike other technologies, which increase the productivity of a worker, the robot actually replaces the worker. That is the primary purpose in building robots (Scott, 1985; Draper, 1985). Draper (46) notes:

> Besides, as T.A. Heppenheimer, one of Minsky's contributors points out, they (robots) "didn't get bored, take vacations, qualify for pensions, or leave soft-drink cans rattling around inside the assembled products. They ... would accept heat, radioactivity, poisonous fumes, or loud noise, all without filing a grievance." Furthermore, they could work round-the-clock without malingering, going to the toilet, or blowing their noses, and were therefore more productive than any human worker, and one man or woman could often supervise several robots. The increase in output per hour was potentially enormous.

The robotic revolution that penetrated the automobile industry -- and has contributed to a generation of practical experience and the development of a knowledge base that helps cut costs and the risks of failure -- is rapidly being extended to other areas. The electronics industry has undergone a major transformation, in that robots are already widely used to assemble finished products (Draper, 1985:48):

About nine tenths of Apple's Macintosh computer, for example, is assembled automatically -- in part by equipment purchased from IBM. This astonishing feat is of deep importance. Welding and painting occur in many industries but the assembly of machines and other products is much more widespread, and it accounts for the largest single share of industrial workers and manufacturing costs. The experts agree that by the middle of the next decade it will be the most important application in robotics. In the meantime, assembly already occupies nearly 20 percent of the robots in Japan, where some electronics manufacturers claim that they have automated one half to three quarters of their assembly operations....

Not long ago the tomato growers of California hired 40,000 migrant workers a year to pick their crop. Then they started using a robot called the Tomato Harvester, and by the start of the 1980s they required only about eight thousand laborers to pick a crop three times as large. This was a fairly difficult application, too, for the modern commercial tomato, although hard, is less hard than most of the objects that robots manipulate, and tomatoes in general tend to be irregular in shape and to grow at unpredictable locations on the vine.

The area of robotics, like so many other areas, is dominated by large companies and networks of engineers and research institutes. The major producers are Unimation (owned by Westinghouse), General Electric, Fanuc of Japan in a joint venture with General Motors Robotics, along with Bendix, Renault, Volkswagen, United Technologies and IBM (Draper, 1985). Draper (48) suggests:

These large companies are making such investments because they know something that the rest of us do not. They know that whatever may be happening at any particular moment, robotics, like the steam engine and electricity, is destined to be part of an industrial revolution. This Third Industrial Revolution will fuse design, manufacture, and marketing into a single stream of information that will eventually permit us to automate just about anything we do not want to do ourselves.

Clearly, there are opposing perspectives, diverse facts to be considered, and contradictory assessments. The differing orientations are typically not engaged in systematic discussion and debate. Nor are they involved in the development of common data bases and shared understandings about what is currently happening and what spectrum of future scenarios is possible or desirable. While we tend to agree with those who argue that the micro-electronic revolution, and in particular the development of robotics and computerized offices systems, will disrupt individual expectations, families, work life, and occupational relationships as well as entire communities and regions, the essential point is that the revolution is controversial. It is a potential issue or set of issues that call for systematic public discussion and assessment.

Finally, we should remember that the micro-electronic revolution is only one in a complex of technological revolutions that have begun -- and will continue -- to transform work, occupational structures, employment conditions, consumption patterns, leisure, whole societies, and the relations among societies.

2.5   TECHNOLOGICAL CHANGE AND POLITICS

Since the 1960s there has been growing concern about the impacts of technological innovation and development on the environments in which we live and on the quality of life. Changing perceptions and assessments have emerged with respect to resource limits, pollution, work life, and employment, as well as other areas of social life. In a number of Western societies there have emerged strategic groups -- green movements and parties -- struggling for pollution control, protection of the environment, and changes in social values and life styles. They refuse to accept unrestrained technological development. They attempt to set forth, not necessarily successfully, new demands and constraints relating to modern technologies and their development.

Still, social learning about -- and increased politicalization of -- technological development has taken place. This has led more and more to the recognition that:

1. Technological innovations and the development of sociotechnical systems not only produce positive, intended effects but also have negative consequences for the environment, for working conditions and employment, and for social life generally. Many of the impacts are unanticipated or unintended. As Camilleri (1976:222) has argued:

> Inventions and discoveries in such fields as medicine, communication and transport may have revolutionized man's relationship with the natural order, but they have at the same time made him the victim of these new forms of power. What is in question is not the misuse of power, widespread though it is, but the disparity in power which enables a small minority of bureaucrats, planners and engineers to establish their technocratic rule over millions of men, and one dominant age to achieve mastery over gener-

ations yet unborn. It is not that this new race of conditioners is composed of evil men but that they have undermined their own humanity and that of their subjects by their very decision to shape humanity. In this sense, both the conditioners and the conditioned have been reduced to artifacts. Far from subduing reality to the wishes of men, the technical process of conditioning risks producing "the abolition of man."

2. The benefits and negative impacts may be experienced in different time frames, and some may be purely potentialities that cannot be excluded. The immediately obvious costs may apppear quite small in comparison with the intended benefits. But in the case of complex sociotechnical systems, the process of learning about and assessing consequences may be a long, difficult enterprise. As Martino (1972) has pointed out, it is the unintended (and often unanticipated) consequences that frequently show up as costs, but that have failed to be considered from the outset. By the time they are recognized, the technology is all too well entrenched amid vested interests and organizational and physical infra-structures, and appears impossible or far too costly to replace (the problem of apparent "irreversibility").

3. The benefits and "costs" of technologies and technological development are usually distributed unequally among groups and segments of society -- as well as among generations, in the latter case leaving as a heritage a polluted, unattractive environment and shattered community structures.

4. Individuals, groups, organizations, and social movements react to the impacts of modern technologies and technological developments, particularly large-scale ones. This may be in response to distributional effects, to environmental damage, to the depletion of resources and pollution, to the loss of jobs or meaningful work, or to the declining quality of the

work environment or everyday life. Some citizen or interest groups react also on grounds of "due process" or the principle that they should be able to participate in and influence the decisions and developments affecting their lives and the lives of their children.

In democratic societies, the general public and public-interest groups have certain rights to participate -- directly or indirectly -- in major decisions and to influence change, such as the changes relating to the introduction and development of major new technologies. Such decisions may be made to a greater or lesser extent through markets or through decision-making processes internal to an industry or key consumer groups. But even markets can be subject to public scrutiny and regulation.

New values, greater political awareness, and social learning about technological change -- and its potential impacts on the social and natural environment -- have made it increasingly difficult (at least in the European democracies), to simply introduce "technical solutions," particularly large-scale ones. In some instances, tough questions are being raised. In today's world there are normative and political pressures to consider non-economic and non-technical goals and values in the assessment, choice, and development of technology. One such consideration concerns the extent to which a technology or family of technologies is "environmentally friendly," that is, the extent to which it is compatible with environmental protection, the extent to which it will improve work life and conditions of employment; or the extent to which it is compatible with the constitutional order or other core features of a democratic society. Technology need not be selected and developed only in order to realize maximum increases in productivity or economic gain. Selection and development may be guided as well by qualitative, broadly human, and ecological considerations. This may become more and more the case in the future.

Much of the discontent and occasional open conflict relating to modern technologies and their development result from a failure of designers, planners, and policymakers to allow affected groups to express their diverse values and concerns and to exercise influence *early in the design or planning stages at a time when the decisions may be more readily reversed or reformulated in quite different ways. This is particularly important in the case of projects and developments which are on a large scale and have long time frames.* Of course, involvement of currently active groups is no guarantee against future problems and crisis. New groups may emerge. Some established groups or unorganized citizens may come to change their viewpoints about, or assessments of, a development. However, early public discussion and genuine attempts to determine what developments appear technically and economically feasible as well as politically and culturally feasible would be a major step in the right direction.

That process of public review is consistent with the principle advanced here that *technological development is a social learning process as well as an enterprise in the collective structuring of social life.* In the course of such processes, social agents -- whether individuals, groups, or organizations -- acquire knowledge and reformulate their goals, strategies, and engagements. New concepts, shifts in values, and changes in the relevant "rules of the game" and social institutions will be reflected sooner or later in technological developments. Often, these changes occur at a slower pace than the more purely technical or engineering changes and, occasionally, only after prolonged and costly struggles. The "feedback" associated with technological development is characterized not only by delays, distortion, and confusion, but by barriers. Thus, social assessment and a more human and environmentally considerate shaping of the future may be partially blocked. Social science research has the *potential* to shed light on such barriers and to facilitate social feedback and learning. This might contribute to humanizing -- and "ecologizing" -- technological development to a greater extent than is the case at present.

The humanization of technological change can be realized in part by identifying unarticulated interests and emerging groups as well as by providing a *practical basis for dialogue and debate between opposing interests.* This is not to suggest that conflict can be eliminated, but only that it can be better institutionalized and grounded on more systematic knowledge, allowing possibly for more creative communication and democratic practice.

2.6   CONCLUSION

Technological developments -- such as those associated with the formation of an information society -- have *unintended and, to a considerable extent, uncontrollable consequences:* the transformation of the economy, shifts in strategic functions of society including the relative decline of industry and the emergence of service and knowledge economies, the growth in social power of certain private and public white-collar groups associated with these transformations, and the societal struggle over income distribution in an economy that is stagnating even as it undergoes technological transformation.

The micro-electronic and communications revolutions, in particular, entail the use of new technologies in production as well as in consumption. These become instruments of function as well as of social power and social status. Some class and status divisions are deepened, others transformed. Computer illiteracy promises to be as serious a handicap as language illiteracy.

Often, the more disruptive and damaging impacts of technological development lead governments, at least in democratic societies, to intervene and to try to regulate the development. By evoking such regulative responses, techological development generates not only the direct transformation of rules associated with the production and use of a technology, but indirect transformations that derive from legislation, policy reformulations, and other rule changes that are introduced through administrative and social learning processes.

Growing public concern about the impacts of technological innovations and possible future developments has led in some countries, such as West Germany and the United States, particularly since the late 1960s, to the emergence of demands and political ambitions to shape and regulate major technological developments through democratic processes. However, such demands do not in and of themselves assure that the necessary expert knowledge and institutional capacities are available to achieve democratic direction according to new goals and policies.

Paradoxically, in the modern welfare states of Europe and North America, there is considerable insecurity and alienation because (a) technological transformations alter work and employment conditions as well as life styles and family and community relations and (b) political-administrative responses to the impacts of technological development generate new and often confusing laws, regulations, and agencies -- an entire complex -- to regulate that development and to deal with some of its negative social and environmental consequences. *Hyperchange and overdevelopment result.*

A new logic or rationality should be a major aim of the philosophy and policies concerning technological development. The new logic should be more transparent to the general public and policymakers and should be, in principle, simpler and more coherent. *It should be aimed at establishing "preventive policies and measures" rather than the vast hodgepodge of palliative policies and measures that so characterize the current logic.*

Consciousness about the implications of technological choice and development has grown and, in our view, are likely to continue to grow. The processes of technological design, introduction, and management are being made -- and should continue to be made -- more transparent. Such knowledge would make possible better information spreading and an improvement in public debate and, indeed, would extend public influence over technological design and future development.

Winner (1983), in discussing "fabrication," "the activity through which homo faber strives to erect a durable home on earth," writes:

> Arendt understood that activity of this kind involved the combined work of artists, craftsmen, historians, poets, architects, engineers and constitution makers.... I am suggesting that it is now useful to think about technological design features in roughly the same way that the legislators of the ancient world or the eighteenth-century philosophers pondered the structural characteristics of political constitutions. Technologies provide frameworks of order for the modern world. As such, it now makes sense to try to understand the forms of authority, justice, public-good, and freedom that their order entails.

Chapter 4 suggests forms of democratic organization that can contribute to facilitating an understanding of sociotechnical development and control over it.

NOTES

[1] Indeed, the widespread introduction of computers into homes, factories, business offices, and government has been a *minimal* political issue. In contrast, for instance, to energy and environmental issues, political consciousness is low. Many, if not most, see only advantages. Others consider the development as irrelevant for them or as such a powerful force that they cannot affect or change it.

[2] In connection with this, W. I. Sussman has pointed out that, in large measure, the office and the office building are products of the new communications; they are unthinkable without the telegraph and telephone, the typewriter and business machine, the elevator, and the railroad.

[3] But more. All spheres of social life have been shaped and transformed by the industrial revolution and are now undergoing restructuring in connection with the post-industrial revolutions in technology, as evidenced by changes in music/cultural forms, home production and consumption, the manufacturing as well as the service sectors of a society, farming, politics, and diplomacy, and not least war-making.

[4] Contemporary sociology has had relatively little to say about technology and technological change, even if sociology emerged in connection with the industrial revolution. Weingart (1984:115) points out: "Technique, technology, or more generally artifacts have had no systematic place in Sociological Theory since the modern

theory of action superseded Marx and Durkheim."

In general, the language and analytic framework that sociology and the other social sciences have available to investigate and analyze the social context of objects, physical artifacts, and the physical world in their social contexts are at present very limited.

[5] A related issue that can be raised here concerns the implications of technologies for the creation and perpetuation of social rules and social organization. In considering technology in connection with social action, we find it useful to distinguish between the artifacts themselves, the activities involved in managing and using them, and the social principles and rules governing their management and use. The same artefact may serve, on the one hand, as an instrument to effectively achieve certain product-making or object-transforming effects and, on the other, as a symbol of authority or even worship. In the latter case, we note, for instance, an instrument such as a sword and imposing structures such as the Empire State Building or a nuclear power facility.

Nevertheless, the two systems and their related practices correspond to different "social forms," with quite distinct logics. One is oriented to concrete, material effects. The other is oriented to maintaining or reinforcing a social relationship with differences in authority and power. The two logics may be fully compatible or complementary, but not necessarily so (Burns and Flam, 1987).

[6] As with social action generally, human agents develop and apply elaborate rules around the use of technologies: knowledge rules, value and action or normative rules. Indeed, the design of technologies presupposes such social rule systems on the part of those who use them. At the same time, technologies such as machines are "systems of action" *incorporating rules in their de-*

sign (see Perrow, 1979). In this sense, a technology, even a simple one such as a door key, entails an institutional frame, implicit social rule systems to regulate the use of the key in locking and unlocking one or more doors where principles of property rights, technical rules, informal rules agreed on by friends and neighbors, as well as a number of unwritten rules operate. (We are grateful to Bernward Joerges, Wissenschaftszentrum, Berlin, for this observation).

The sociotechnical systems built up around a major technology such as the motorcar (roads, fuel distributive system, drive-in movies, motels, shopping centers, etc.) make certain actions and transactions possible at the same time that others become exceedingly complicated or impossible (Winner, 1983).

[7] Engineers and designers are a strategic group engaged in rule formation relating to the design of technology and sociotechnical systems. Also important in this connection are those such as managers, engineers, and workers who decide on the concrete utilization of technology (and therefore on the implementation as well as reformulation of rule systems relating to the use of new technology in concrete task or activity settings).

[8] On the one hand, applications of science have obviously played a major role in the development of aircraft, rockets, etc. On the other hand, technical developments such as the steam engine led to the progress of scientific knowledge.

[9] Discussing the social limits on the application of science to technology, Rosenberg (1982:42) writes:

> Science itself can never be extensively applied to the productive process so long as that process continues to be dependent upon

forces the behavior of which cannot be predicted and controlled with the strictest accuracy. Science, in other words, must incorporate its principles in *impersonal* machinery. Such machinery may be relied upon to behave in accordance with scientifically established physical relationships. Science, however, cannot be incorporated into technologies dominated by large-scale human interventions because human action involves too much that is subjective and capricious. More generally, human beings have wills of their own and are therefore too refractory to constitute reliable, that is, controllable inputs in complex and interdependent productive processes.

The decisive step, then, was the development of a machine technology that was not heavily dependent upon human skills or volitions, where the productive process was broken down into a series of separately analysable steps. The historic importance of the manufacturing system was that it had provided just such a breakdown. The historic importance of modern industry was that it incorporated these separate steps into machine processes to which scientific knowledge and principles could now be routinely applied. "The principle, carried out in the factory system, of analysing the process of production into its constituent phases and of solving the problems thus proposed by the application of mechanics, of chemistry, and of the whole range of natural sciences, becomes the determining principle everywhere" (Marx). When this stage has been reached, Marx argues, technology becomes for the first time capable of indefinite improvement.

[10] Engineers, designers, and managers may easily mis-judge the ease with which a technology can be "introduced." Those groups who see their occupations or jobs threatened may exaggerate the difficulties. Typically, the outcomes are complicated. However, the point is that often there is a well-developed, frequently covert politics to technological innovation and development (see Burns, 1985; Baumgartner and Burns, 1984; Baumgartner et al., 1986).

[11] In the United States, for instance, 1.7 jobs on the average in day-shift plants were eliminated for each first-generation robot, and 2.7 on the average in round-the-clock plants. Second-generation units are expected to result in a much larger net elimination, to be followed by third-, fourth-, and fifth- generation robotics.

3

SCIENCE AND POLITICS: STUDIES IN COMPETING LOGICS

3.1 INTRODUCTION: APPLIED SCIENCE AND POLICYMAKING

In modern Western societies there are serious obstacles to effectively organizing democratic public discussion, particularly when the issues concern science and technology:

1. Most citizens and their representatives feel ignorant and incompetent in engaging in discussions of such issues. Although political representatives are convinced that they should have a say about such matters, they feel it especially difficult to engage themselves in a competent manner.

2. Engineers, scientists, and other technical experts tend to dominate the process, defining the technical issues, evaluation criteria. and procedures. Or, in collusion with key political agents, they remove the basic discussion of such issues from public deliberation, defining them as "technical" in character.

3. The public, and its representative bodies, are involved, if at all, only in the final phase of approving or legitimizing decisions, plans, and programs relating to such issues.

4. Typically, genuine alternatives to a proposed policy, plan, or program are not formulated. A single alternative is presented[1]. Or, at best, when less preferred alternatives are also presented along with the preferred option, the former are, in the typical case, poorly or unsystematically spelled out in terms of their many-sided features. Their disadvantages are stressed. Potential advantages compared to the alternative preferred by an elite or a dominating majority -- with the backing of technical expertise -- are ignored or downplayed.

Scientists and other technical experts are frequently involved in the arena of political decision making, especially concerning economic, educational, and technological isuses. Many of them are associated with one or more points of view or political interests. This applies also to the natural sciences and engineering, as recent issues related to nuclear power, the breeder reactors, genetic engineering, and SDI (Strategic Defense Initiative) have pointed up. Science and technical expertise are an integral part of technocratic decision making in modern society.

Is the involvement of scientists and engineers in such matters a part of their professional activity or a part of their activities as citizens? Or is it both? If it is both, and expertise and politics cannot be systematically separated, then what mixture is appropriate and how is such a mixture to be organized and regulated?

In this regard Douglas and Wildavsky (1982:49; 63-64) point out:

> Scientists disagree on whether there are problems, what solutions to propose, and if intervention will make things better or worse. One scientist thinks of Mother Nature as merely secreting a healthy amount of dirt and another thinks of her being forced to ingest lethal pollutants. No wonder the ordinary lay person has difficulty in followng the argument, and no wonder the sci-

entists have difficulty presenting themselves in public.

If the lack of agreement among scientists is due to absence of knowledge, as information increases, disputes would decrease. On the other hand, better measurement opens more possibilities, (and) more research brings more ignorance to the light of day. The tendency toward confrontation instead of disputation may be due to the kind of questions asked, questions that do not permit of widely acceptable answers.

They raise a fundamental question:

When scientists debate among themselves issues involving risk, are they better able than others to separate scientific from political issues, to say what science says, or to apply it to public policy? They ought to be able to make the issues more manageable or the debate less acrimonious. Presumably they can quantify costs and benefits or agree on an estimate of the dangers. Insofar as the risks are physical, scientists might come closer to agreement either on what they know or what they do not know, for example, the hazards of low-dose exposures. But if the perception of risks is social, rooted in cultural bias, scientists should behave much the same as other mortals. Some scientific conclaves seem to be very like political contests, except that the participants are not limited by being held responsible for what they say. (p.61)

Certainly, many scientists and other experts, including social scientists, advocate their viewpoints *as a part of or through their science.* Edward Teller, the nuclear physicist, is a wonderful example of this breed. Time and time again he has spoken out publically on behalf of those at the Pentagon who push for new, revolutionary weapon systems. On the one hand, he is in a position to understand alternatives, certainly better than a the average politician without the same depth of scientific expertise. He fails to honestly formulate or articulate *alternative* positions. He presents his own or a Pentagon group's position with dramatic arguments and with the full authority of scientific expertise. This is not science, however; it is the political wolf draped in the sheepskin of science[2].

Max Weber, the great German sociologist (1864-1920), argued that politics, and the values motivating politics, should be kept separate from scientific activity[3]. However, in many instances of interaction of scientists with practitioners and policymakers, the boundary between scientific research and practical action is difficult to define precisely and to maintain. This is particularly a problem with applied and policy research, which is the concern of this chapter. Scientific and other forms of expertise are often introduced in order to gain support for or to legitimize political decisions or policies. That is, expertise becomes a political resource, subject to powerful ideological influences and political rules of the game. These encounters often give rise to a great deal of ambiguity. Technical and scientific norms and validity are vulnerable and may be readily subverted under such conditions.

The institutional forms of activity governing scientists, on the one hand, and politicians or policymakers, on the other, are in principle different. In some respects, they are contradictory[4]. Clark and Majone (1984:7-8) point out that, in general, the engagement of professions and other groups in different social roles implies the use of diverse criteria in the evaluation of scientific results, and this explains in part some of the misunderstandings and conflicts that arise when, for instance, applied science meets politics:

(A)n academic statistician, a company expert and a Congressional staffer will use different criteria to evaluate a study on the coincidence of cancer deaths and particular occupations. Their conflicting judgements of the study will not be resolved by reference to less uncertain or more clearly presented data. *Required instead is a mutual comprehension of the different critical perspectives being employed.*

That different critical appraisals are arrived at by people in different roles is not a bad thing as such. It may simply reflect different needs and concerns of different segments of society, or different degrees of freedom in making certain key methodological choices. So long as the judgements leveled from the perspective of one particular role are not presented or misinterpreted as judgements relevant to or speaking for all possible roles, we have a healthy state of pluralistic criticism. Difficulties begin to arise when this neat partitioning of roles and the criticism voiced from them begins to break down. Unfortunately, such breakdowns seem more the rule than the exception in actual practice.

The issues that arise when science, technology, and public policy-making meet are typically trans-scientific. The issues may be formulated in the language of science but cannot, either in principle or practice, be addressed or assessed in purely scientific terms. The logic of trans-scientific issues, for example, deciding safety standards for a nuclear reactor or deciding acceptable risk levels, is different from that of conventional scientific practice.

In the following sections, we shall focus attention, first, on particular modes of organizing transactions between applied scientists and politicians and other practitioners in policy settings, and, second, on the dilemmas, confusion, and conflicts that arise in these transactions. The first two sections focus on certain relevant problems arising as a result of engaging scientists and other types of experts in policy processes. The last section discusses some of the implications of our analysis for policy and applied research.

3.2   SCIENCE AND POLITICS

The close coupling of much scientific activity to politics has become typical of the modern world. This is a result of sustained efforts to harness science to national political interests -- interests not limited simply to military considerations. Wittrock points out the importance of this development and some of the dilemmas and tensions this has engendered (1984:8):

> During the 20th century and particularly after the Second World War, governments have increasingly tried to link up science to national aims and public policies as well as to tap it as a source of economic growth. The role of applied science as a commodity and tool has brought the scholarly world infinitely greater resources in the period after the Second World War than every before in its history. But it (applied science) has also tended to undermine its identity and its guiding norms. The translation of science into power, policy and wealth can more adequately be described in terms of processes of bargains than of threats. But the bargains have involved a Faustian element. They have not only provided sufficient leverage to permit large-scale research projects. The entrepreneurs and "condottiere"

which epitomize these undertakings do not conform to the noble norms of an international scientific aristocracy, and the cherished value of openness has been intimately linked to the existence of such an aristocracy. Instead, competition between short-lived project groups is conducive to disruptions in the free flow of information and to efforts to exclude others from it....

Sheldon Rothblatt observes that "the marketability of science" and "the desire of powerful industrial states to employ science in the service of national aims ...may virtually be accepted as constants, and scientists have always been of two minds about it." However, in the last two decades efforts have been intensified all over the Western world to use research as a limitless factor of production to promote growth and to pull economies out of slump and stagnation, as a cure-all guide to policies for social betterment and welfare, and as a rational basis for policies to trim bureaucracy and increase efficiency. Not only may these efforts have highlighted an inherent tension in an established pattern of accomodating universalistic norms and particularistic commitments in modern universities and research institutions. These efforts have also revealed tensions and inconsistencies in many of the fundamental conceptions underlying science policies of recent years.

In modern society, public decisions are made according to one or more legitimation criteria, including that of scientific validity. These consist of rules and principles for assessing the rationality of a decision. Referring to the "Will of God" or to "destiny" is illegitimate in modern, Western societies. A decision should be justified in terms of its contribution to legitimate objectives, its likely effectiveness, its compatibility with law or administrative procedure.

Two general types of principles for assessing the legitimacy of social decision-making have been distinguished by Simon (1977; also see Kickert, 1979). The first type refers to the *content of the decision* ("substantive rationality"). Such legitimation is based on the use of technical sciences, economics, and other branches of systematic knowledge. A proposition or decision is legitimized if it is consistent with, for instance, economic or engineering knowledge. The second type refers to collective decision-making procedures ("procedural rationality"). The organizing principle of parliamentary decision making, for example, defines what decisions are legitimate in terms of the *procedure that is followed, irrespective of counter-indications* of technical expertise or anticipated consequences. A parliamentary majority decision for building nuclear plants or hydropower facilities may be *procedurally and legally rational at the same time that it may conflict with other rationality principles.* For instance, the decision may be judged to be unsound economically or environmentally, or because of security considerations, although in reaching it, established legal and political procedures were followed.

The various logics applied to the social process of organizing and legitimizing public decisions are neither consistent nor complete. They leave play for maneuvering and negotiation among those involved in the transactions. On the one hand, economic reasoning may lead to the conclusion that, for example, investment in alternative energy sources or in conservation provides for greater returns than continuation of nuclear investment programs. On the other hand, the decision to continue with the nuclear programs may be based on the legitimacy of parliamentary democracy: parliament and the political leadership have expressed their will or the general will in a formal decision, namely, legislation. Yet another principle for legitimizing the decision may be based on the degree of general public acceptance. Thus, while a decision is formally legitimate according to the institutionalized rules of parliamentary democracy, resistance to the decision from citizen groups and local communities might be so high that the decision cannot be effectively implemented. In such a case popular acceptance, or opposition, although *formally* not a valid legitimation base in a parliamentary democracy, may become another criterion for choosing or justifying decisions (see Offe, 1983; Meyer-Abich, 1984:292).

In sum, public policy-making and planning entail the activation *of multiple legitimation bases.* These bases are coupled to different institutional segments of society and professional groups. They have different rationalities consisting of systems of rules for evaluating decisions before, during, and after decision making and implementation. They do not,however, present unambiguous and clear-cut recipes for making or justifying decisions. The contradictions between different rationalities and the ambiguity of rationality rules open the way not only for conflict and for various types of negotiation and political games. The games themselves may lead to the activation or formulation of principles or "meta-rules" for handling competing logics of action. (Meta-rules are rules about rules, in particular rules dealing with diverse, even contradictory rule systems. We discuss this notion in more detail later in this chapter.) Clark and Majone (1984:33) observe:

> Two overriding questions asked regarding policymaking in open societies are its efficacy in solving practical problems and its responsiveness to popular control. As C. E. Lindblom remarks, however, these questions lead to "a deep conflict (that) runs through common attitudes to policymaking. On the one hand, people want policy to be informed and well analyzed. On the other hand, they want policymaking to be democrat-

ic.... In slightly different words, on the one hand they want policymaking to be more scientific; on the other, they want it to remain in the world of politics.

The results of scientific inquiry performed in policy contexts is a potential source of political power. The question therefore arises, as it does regarding any source of power, of what constitutes its legitimate use. In appraising efforts to provide usable knowledge through scientific inquiry we must therefore finally consider criteria of legitimacy.

Scientific analyses and results are often used in modern society as a basis for justifying or legitimizing public decisions, a pattern that many studies of the relationship between policy-oriented research and public policy-making point up. Clark and Majone (1984:35) stress this function:

The social uses of science have always had something in common with the social uses of religion. And in the two decades following the Second World War, modern science took on a most religious-looking numinous legitimacy as an unquestioned source of authority on all manner of policy problems.

As inputs to policy and planning processes, scientific knowledge and analysis contribute to defining and organizing "images of reality" and programs of action. In such ways, they influence problem definitions, solutions proposed, and the perceived legitimacy of political proposals and policies.

Science can be conceived as a social logic -- or institutionalized system of rules -- for defining the rationality of a proposition, conclusion, or decision. The rule frame (including methodological rules and procedures) is maintained and developed by "scientific communities"[5]. Different scientific paradigms, and the institutions in which they are embodied, imply somewhat different rule frames.

Scientific paradigms have to compete with other rationality bases as well as with each other. Substantive scientific rationality may compete or clash with legal and political forms of rationality, as in administrative and political settings where "non-scientific" concepts of evidence, truth, analysis, logical argument, and certainty are valid. Science is one competing input among many (Bulmer, 1986). At the same time, two or more scientific paradigms may compete with one another in areas related to policy-making, such as reductionist and contextualist thinking in biology (cf. Krimsky, 1982:380; Kollek, 1986), or monetarism and Keynesianism in economics.

The influence possibilities -- and in general the role -- of science in policy-making tend to vary according to the policy problem and characteristics of the policy process.[6]) In relatively simple and orderly decision-making processes with clear goals and well-defined participants, one may readily apply clear-cut, established rules -- although these need not necessarily be scientifically based -- in making decisions and in justifying the decisions made. In complicated decision processes, where goals are ambiguous and where there are a large number of participants with substantially different institutional affiliations and legitimation bases, scientific rationality or rationalities have to compete with other legitimation bases. In such a situation, some or all of the interests may try to mobilize scientific analyses and conclusions to support their positions. This is well exemplified in the debates about nuclear energy and genetic engineering in a number of countries.

In some instances, science becomes a basis for political discourse and legitimacy. It serves, then, as a common means for "determining truth," formulating arguments, drawing conclusions, and making collective decisions.

(Whether or not this is justified in all instances, it has, nevertheless, a concrete effect on processes of policy-making and acceptance).

Clark and Majone (1984), drawing on Wildavsky and Tennenbaum (1981), provide an illustration of the complex interplay between researchers and politicians -- and also some of the ways by which biases readily enter into scientific judgments. The case concerned scientific advice regarding the question, "What is the size of America's remaining oil and gas reserves":

> The NRC (National Research Council) showed that serious scientific studies of the question had produced estimates spanning an order of magnitude, and that government (U.S. Geological Survey) estimates tended to be two to three times the size of industry estimates. The NRC itself concluded that the most reasonable estimate was less than half the most recent USGS figure, and only slightly larger than those proposed by industry experts. (Clark and Majone, 1984:9-11,18)

In the course of a congressional inquiry, one NRC committee member admitted "(E)stimates of future supplies of oil and gas are so dependent upon unknown scientific factors and unknown environmental and political factors as to be almost unknowlable." Clark and Majone (1984:10-11,18) observe:

> These "almost unknowable" estimates were nonetheless published to three significant figures by the NRC with no uncertainty ranges. How were the particular NRC values arrived at? According to another NRC committee member, "from our point of view, we thought it advisable ...to accept more conservative estimates, think-

ing that most of the Geological Survey estimates are relatively high, and most of the oil company estimates relatively conservative." As Wildavsky and Tennenbaum ask in their review of the case, "This is science?".

Congress wanted "a number," and the National Research Council therefore gave them "a number," even though committee members acknowledged in their testimony that it was little more than guesswork -- i.e. nothing like the consensually certified knowledge that its trappings and origins implied. Similar examples, of which perhaps the most notorious would involve the willingness of scientists to deliver cost-benefit assessments of long-term and large-scale environmental changes, could easily be cited.

They conclude (1984:18):

> (I)t is clear that there existed virtually no overlap in the critical criteria underlying the three different evaluations of the oil and gas studies. Whatever more fundamental disagreements may have existed regarding the worth of the studies, most of the conflict in the hearing room can be traced to the different critical standards being employed by different critics.

In applied and policy research, where scientists interact with practitioners, the motives and actions of the researcher are often subject to non-scientific norms and influence. In part they become dependent on, and therefore open to the influence of, other types of actors in the various phases of research activity. Also, researchers may be tempted to actively engage in the political game of trying to persuade, influence, or countervail other actors. In general, applied science settings expose researchers to multiple reference groups: the research community, including institutions of higher education and research, and the groups of practitioners or policymakers (in many instances the various groups or agents have incompatible conceptions of and demands on applied researchers).

The principles of neither of science, nor of politics indicate how researchers are to resolve contradictory demands and cross-pressures. In the absence of relatively well-defined norms and guidelines, behavior will be confused, equivocating, or vascillating. Clark and Majone (1984:3-4) stress:

> Study after study gleefully demonstrates that scientific inquiry in policy contexts is shot through with "fatal" methodological flaws, "hidden" biases, erroneous data, or trivial intent. To cite only some of the most readily accessible examples, works by Ida Hoos, D. B. Lee, and Gary Brewer delivered the flow critical to early social system studies; Quade and Cline to military analysis; Ackerman and Fiering to water resource management; Hutchinson, Loasby and Henry for economic forecasting; and Arthur and Sanderson for systems studies of Third World development. The publication of Donella Meadow's *Groping in the Dark* has left the global modeling community in such scholarly rout that only the military seems willing to fund it. Most recently, *Policy Sciences* has entertained its readers with an "expose" of the shortcomings of IIASA's analyses of energy policy (IIASA = International Institute of Applied Systems Analysis, Vienna).

They add, however (4), "Missing is any indication that good scientific inquiry in policy contexts might have more appropriate objectives than trying to emulate either pure science or pure democracy." In practice (1):

(S)cientific inquiry cannot discover most things policy makers would like to know. Much of what it does discover remains uncertain or incomplete. How, then, is would-be-scientific knowledge any more reliable a guide to policy than other forms of knowledge, prejudice, or propaganda? Moreover, in practice experts often disagree on what science knows and on what the knowledge means for policy. *But if the knowledge produced by science is not consensual, what special claim for hearing has it in a world of multiple opinions and biases?* (Emphasis added)

Clearly, the misapplication or abuse of science in policy processes puts up for stakes the future legitimacy of scientific knowledge as a policy input -- and even science as a major social institution (Ueberhorst, 1986).

3.3   SCIENTIFIC AND POLITICAL LOGICS

Below we schematically present and compare the social logics of science and politics as bases for the crganization and legitimation of social action and interaction. We also discuss important patterns of interaction between scientists and policymakers and principles for handling inconsistencies between scientific and political action logics.

Scientific Logic

Science, as Merton (1976:32-33) has pointed out, appears as one of the great social institutions, coordinate with the other major institutions of society: the economy, education and religion, the family, and polity. Like other institutions, science has its normative subculture: a body of social rules shared and transmitted by those involved in the institution. The norms and standards define the technically and morally allowable patterns of behavior, indicating what is prescribed, preferred, permitted, or proscribed.

Merton stressed that a scientific community does not have a single, perfectly consistent set of norms[7]. In particular, there are conflicts between sub-communities, schools, and scientific traditions with competing paradigms and methodologies within the field of science. In this chapter, however, we emphasize the *unitary logic of science* as a basic rationality because our aim here is to consider inter-institutional inconsistencies and conflicts between the logics of science and of politics. In the following chapter, we take a more realistic view, considering that contradictions and conflicts between scientific groups may generate problems when organizing political discourse and decision making.

Indeed, some political issues and conflicts start off with conflicts within scientific disciplines. For instance, scientists carry their conflicts over into the public arena in order to gain support or to legitimize their respective positions or to influence policy and legislation. Much of the initial public opposition to President Reagan's Star Wars Program was launched by scientists and engineers who questioned its technical feasibility as well as its desirability. Scientists taking different positions about future research and development in biotechnologies and genetic engineering have also launched public debates and controversies, particularly in West Germany and the United States (Krimsky, 1982; Kollek, Tappeser, and Altner, 1986). Obviously, a realistic political framework cannot ignore contradictions and conflicts *within* scientific and other expert communities, particularly those that relate to major new technological developments. To do so would leave political authority and policy-making without strategies and procedures to respond to such conflicts and, above all, to assure their subordination to the democratic process. This is a matter to which we shall return in the following chapter.

One of the most important aspects of scientific activity concerns the validity of arguments. The rules for such validation are contained in methodology and scientific paradigms. A proposition or argument is considered valid ("true") if it is made in accordance with such rules[8]. In general, scientific statements are to be formulated, and validated either according to procedures of logical argument and/or according to support provided by empirical data. The empirical evidence should be obtained, organized and presented according to established scientific methods and procedures in the discipline[9].

Certain rules, which are quite common in everyday social life, are excluded in genuine scientific communities. For instance, there is neither voting on viewpoints since the majority may well be wrong, nor bargaining over them. "Scientific truth" cannot be negotiated as a compromise between two opinions. In the actual practice of science, of course, such negotiating and compromising go on, as can be seen in the polemics, coalition formation, and politics that take place *within* scientific communities (an indication of the important distinction between "theoretical ideal" and "practice"). However, negotiated settlements and compromises *relating to the "content of science" cannot be professionally or publicly legitimized, even if they go on.*

Political Logic

The rules of politics have a logic or rationality differing from that of the rules of science. These rules serves two purposes: to make decisions politically acceptable and to reduce conflict among the different parties engaged in the decision-making process. "Scientific truth" is not the central issue in defining and constructing social reality in everyday political or social life. *The acceptability of a certain reality to the different parties with their particular interests is of much greater importance.*

The great differences in the logics of action based on the rules of science (S) and the rules of politics (P) are pointed up in the use of language and forms of communication. Ideally, in science one uses clear methods, evidence defined as scientific, and explicit language in terms of well-defined concepts. The scientist qualifies statements or makes probabilistic ones as a reflection of the level of uncertainty about the statements' validity or reliability.

In contrast, politics often entails the strategic use of vague or equivocating statements as well as contradictory formulations in order to *actually maintain or increase ambiguity.* The ambiguity is required in order to maintain a basis for future acceptance. In democratic politics, politicians compete for people's votes. They are rewarded with power and leadership opportunities by gaining votes, not necessarily by clarifying issues. In many settings, they want to appeal to as many people as possible or to avoid serious conflicts and maintain the freedom of action to negotiate with other political actors at a later stage.

At the same time, politicians or policymakers often request from scientists clear, unequivocating statements in order to support their arguments or proposals[10]. (Indeed, the most common notion of science among politicians is that of a "black box" which, when called upon, produces clear-cut reports, data, analyses, and proposals). Such political requirements are usually not readily consistent with scientific norms calling for care in the use and manipulation of data and in the formulation of conclusions.

"Reality" and "truth" are, according to the rules of politics, *negotiable in a certain sense.* The negotiation aims at political or public acceptance and the resolution of conflicts.

At the same time, policymakers often know that a current false statement about social phenomena, at least by scientific standards, may become true by pronouncing it true, as suggested by the following figure (Merton, 1957; Henshel, 1978; among others):

```
STATEMENT ==> AUTHORITATIVE  ===> INFLUENCE  ==> STATEMENT
P IS FALSE   (e.g., scientific) on SOCIAL      P IS TRUE
             PRONOUNCEMENTS      ACTION
             ABOUT PHENOMENA
             TO WHICH P REFERS
```

Figure 1: RESTRUCTURING REALITY

As a result of such strategic possibilities, scientific and technical arguments and "truths" become political resources that can and are used in gaining acceptance for a policy or program and "making a difference in the world." *Certainly, the logic of "making truth" differs from the logic of "discovering truth."*

Another area of very different behavior concerns the publication of data. The rules of science presuppose considerable openness, whereas those of politics usually imply highly selective barriers for the transfer and dissemination of information. Open exchange of information could easily result in conflicts or blocked positions that are difficult to manage, or open exchange could provide advantages to opponents in political competition or struggles. Policymakers often want to have full access to certain kinds of scientific knowledge as a strategic resource in their games and actions, but oppose its publication in the belief that their competitors or opponents could exploit it for their own purposes. Thus, the systematic withholding or releasing of information becomes a strategy in its own right, legitimating and de-legitimating policies and public decisions.

The institutions of both science and politics *contain rules for information selection and organization.* Politics implies information selection and organization according to rules of political expedience and compromise. Controversial or conflicting information is often avoided in the interest of gaining acceptance of, for example, particular definitions of problems and formulations of strategic space.

Scientific rules and methods are also highly selective with respect to what is considered valid information and argument. Moreover, there are normative pressures and reputational incentives to identify inconsistencies and gaps in information and arguments. This is part of the sustained, internal dynamics of modern science.

The rule systems of both science and of politics exclude and select, *but they do so on different grounds and in different ways.* Nevertheless, points of convergence may occur, providing policymakers with an opportunity to exploit the rules of *scientific exclusion and selection for policymakers' own political or governance purposes.* In addition, some scientists are prepared to use such points of convergence for their own professional (and personal) interests. In particular, support of a certain policy line or argument by a scientific group is exchanged for political support or public funds with which research institutes and schools of thought can be financed and developed.

In sum, *science and politics entail two distinct action logics and rationality types.* Interactions between scientists and policymakers open up possibilities for politicians and scientists to compromise the integrity of scientific discipline and/or for scientists to misappropriate the legitimate role of politicians in a democratic society, which is to determine ground rules, policies, and conditions that shape and reshape future developments, including technological futures.

Meta-rules for Handling Conflicts between Systems S and P

The interplay between scientific and political logics is especially apparent in the case of much policy research, research consultation, and applied science in general. When politicians and scientists interact in their respective roles, the two sets of rules, S and P, are activated at the same time. This may give rise to uncertainty and conflict. Uncertainty and conflict arising in the interactions are handled typically by higher-order rules and principles or *meta-rules*. These reconcile contradictions by, for instance, giving precedence to one or the other system, or they may indicate some possible synthesis. Policymakers and scientists "negotiate" -- or have previously negotiated with each other -- about the operating meta-rules. The latter are typically informal and even implicit in character. The resolution of these questions often takes place in conjunction with the selection by policymakers of scientists or research groups with whom the politicians feel comfortable on the basis of the professional styles or ideology of those selected.

Habermas (1971) distinguishes three modes of social decision-making involving scientific and technical expertise and politics.

1. In the *decisionistic mode,* science is subordinated to politics, possibly leading to ill-informed decisions concerning technical problems and the risks involved. Such decisions may set in motion physical, biological, and social processes whose outcomes, if they had been foreseen, would be considered undesirable by many or most of those involved or affected.

2. In the *technocratic mode,* politics is subordinated to technical analysis and to the assumptions and values (often implicit) of scientific and technical elites. The values and concerns of major groups affected by the decisions are neglected. This not only violates elementary principles of democracy but is also highly riskfilled, since important human values and lifeforms are often ignored in a relatively closed process of technological design and development.

3. The *pragmatic mode* integrates public values and scientific knowledge. Habermas suggests that this mode is characterized by unconstrained debate about policy, with no individual or group able to wield power beyond the validity of their arguments (also see Dietz, 1987). Unfortunately, Habermas does not provide any guidance as to how such a mode can be organized or how modern societies can move from the current mix of technocratic and decisionistic modes to a pragmatic mode (Dietz, 1987: 60), a task to which we shall return in Chapter 4.

If a decisionistic mode prevails, the "logic of politics" will dominate applied science and policy research. *Consensus decision-making, negotiated outcomes or majority vote will reflect the logic of political feasibility and legitimacy, rather than that of scientific validity.* In a democracy, majority rule applies in some cases, while in others a unanimous decision rule applies along with various procedures for negotiation between a majority and minorities. Voting procedures give rise to "politically defined realities," which often serve useful public functions. However, these procedures do not correspond to the methods and standards of modern science. Of course, the authority of science can contribute to a definition of social reality and to the determination of strategies and the results of analysis. *And these in turn can lead to consensus policies and actions that make a difference in the "real world."*

In general, in policy research dominated by political rules of the game, the norms of scientific research such as free access to and dissemination of information are very likely to be ignored or compromised or applied only in the most symbolic ways. *Such arrangements serve the actual and hidden purposes of the political utilization of the research and its conclusions.* (Pseudo-) scientific arguments are used in order to achieve political acceptance and the legitimation of particular policies and decisions. In some cases, scientific methods are activated and applied in an apparently rigorous manner for the purposes of producing or maintaining a certain definition of reality and excluding or selecting certain policy options. Science becomes part of the machinery designed to achieve political support. For example, in a certain policy context, a well-tested and respected econometric model is proposed as a basis for policy analysis. The proposal and supporting arguments take the form of scientific statements. However, the underlying purpose of the argument is to prevent problem definitions and solutions -- other than those the model can handle -- from entering the political discussion (Baumgartner and Midttun, 1987).

In many policy research settings, the meta-rule(s) reconciling the apparently conflicting rule systems, S and P, rest on a general principle: Publically, scientific rules and methods -- and the authority of scientific knowledge -- are appealed to and applied formally, whereas the *dominant or prevailing informal rule(s) belong to the machinery of political expediency and* acceptance.[11]'

As suggested by the illustrations in the section on Science and Politics, above, the corruption of science is a major risk of policy and applied research. In general, applied and policy research faces a number of pitfalls:

o Much academic policy research, although carried out in splendid isolation according to conventional scientific rules and procedures, is not accessible to or utilizable by policymakers. This may be the typical case.

o When policy research is primarily designed to contribute to political acceptance, it may largely serve to legitimize policies rather than to elucidate substantive issues and serious problems.

o The stress on political acceptance jeopardizes scientific norms and quality. In the extreme case, the research contributes to the formation of "myths of policy science."

Political acceptance is, of course, a legitimate goal of policy and applied research in democratic societies. The questions that concern us are "What roles shall policy and applied research play in consensus and acceptance processes, and What are the risks to the institutions of politics and science of their close mutual engagement?

3.4   DILEMMAS OF POLICY AND APPLIED RESEARCH

Analytically, one may distinguish several types of relationships between scientific communities and policymakers (see Baumgartner and Midttun, 1987). In an extreme case the community has no dealings or communication with policymakers or other actors influencing policy processes. In some cases the relationship may be a diffuse one in which, for instance, one or more research groups formulate analyses or forecasts that they report by publication and mass media presentations. To the extent that actors important to the policy process receive this information and act on it, the predictions would be of political importance -- they make a difference. More intimate and established forms of exchange and coordination between experts and policymakers are observable in scientific councils directly linked to political parties, parliamentary bodies, and agencies of government[12].

Douglas and Wildavsky (1982:64) note that scientists are not merely paid members of the scientific community, but often political agents. They add:

> Some scientists have been personally so impressed with the gravity of the issues that they have emerged from the laboratories to lend the authority of science to political lobbies... They too have become polarized, inevitably, given the shortage of facts, between the risk takers and the risk averse. Dorothy Nelkin writes: "A striking feature of the new scientific activism is the public nature of its activities and the willingness of activists to engage in and, indeed, to abet political controversy. Disputes among scientists are normally resolved within the scientific community using well-established provisions of collegial review. However, recently, scientists appear willing to air grievances in a political forum -- through the mass media, litigation, or appeals to citizens' groups or political representatives. Citizen participation is sought today for a different reason -- as a means to increase the political accountability of science. While activists in the 1940s fought against political control over research, their recent counterparts -- by calling public attention to conflicts of interest within the scientific community -- seek to increase political control. Such actions have polarized the scientific community, as less radical scientists seek to maintain intact the principles of autonomy and self-regulation that were fought for by activists nearly 30 years ago." Where values are closely compatible and where most facts are agreed upon, attention can be turned to investigating the remaining problems. When values diverge sharply, as in the controversies over risk,

fewer facts are certified and disagreements arise over what used to be taken for granted. In the midst of this severe dissension within the scientific community, efforts arise to save the essence of the activity by moving the demarcation line between between scientific advice and political judgment. By observing where the demarcation line is set -- (whether) more toward science or toward politics -- the degree of dissensus may indirectly be ascertained.

Many of the practitioners of science and technology are naive about or take for granted their overt or covert advocacy roles in modern politics. In this regard Buckley (1973:1) refers to the "ideology of science," citing statements from the address of the retiring president of the the American Association for the Advancement of Science (AAAS), Glen T. Seaborg:

Today we must think of the New World in terms of the entire world, as a community of mankind whose future lies in pursuing the belief that knowledge -- universally obtained, widely shared, and wisely applied -- is the key to the viability of the human race and the earth that supports it.... We are interested in the advancement of science because we know that it will result in the advancement of men.

Buckley comments critically,

Here we find the seeds of ... the "ideology" of science and technology: that it alone or primarily holds the key to human salvation. One acutely problematic phrase in this quote is "wisely applied." Application of any plan of societal scope means decision-making, which means politics, involving a sociocultural context whose forces help structure outcomes one way or another. (p. 1)

Technocratic thinking fits in nicely with bureacratic control and hierarchical structure, whether in its private form in business enterprises or in its public form in government agencies. Together, they advance the idea of "rational action," the belief that all problems have one solution, that conflicts are basically alien to "reason" and "order." Technocracy and bureacracy are foundations of modern rationality and industrial society. Their modes of authority and control tend to dominate or at least compromise democratic processes. Concerning the technocratic conception of a rationally functioning society, Coleman observes (1982:165)[13]:

This model of the locus of policy research in society is one implicitly held by (many researchers and) by most government officials who think of employing policy research.... But its principal characteristic should be recognized: it conceives of information fed back to a single central authority. Its compatibility with bureaucratic theory means also compatibility with a monolithic authority structure. It has no place for a conception of different interests, of democratic political systems in which policy decisions come not from above but from a balance of pressures from conflicting interests.

Our conception of human society and politics is one in which social agents have differing viewpoints, wants, and interests and in which they discuss, negotiate, and struggle with one another, making decisions about the future. In the modern world, these decisions include those based on substantial technical and scientific knowledge. As Coleman (1982:168) suggests:

> (The pluralist conception) regards policy as the resultant of a balance among conflicting values and interests. The other model, the "policymaker-as-rational-actor" model, implicitly assumes that there are no fundamental conflicts of interest, and that when research has clarified the consequences of a policy, conflicts will vanish, or at least that there will be an "objectively correct" policy. The pluralistic mode assumes multiple rational actors, each with differing interests, each with legitimate partial control of policy, and each with needs for information in order to pursue its interests rationally.

In our view, the role of applied science and experts should be institutionalized in such a way as to be consistent with the organizing principles and procedures of democratic discourse. Science and expertise should facilitate the presentation of *sociotechnical or systemic alternatives for the future and for an understanding of the implications. That presentation should enable citizens and politicians to better assess these implications and to contribute, in general, to effective political discussion and* negotiation[14].

This conception is consistent with the notion that *scientific knowledge, and expert knowledge more generally, provide no single objective truth for political decision and future societal* development[15]. This should serve as a point of departure in developing and assessing forms of policy research and policy advice. The contradictions and dilemmas inherent in applied research should be made explicit. Furthermore, upholding the integrity of scientific norms -- and the autonomy of science -- is essential if scientific research is not simply to degenerate into pure politics and the legitimizing of official policies. In the absence of adequate scientific autonomy and internal discipline, scientists engaged in public policy research risk crowning unsound or dubious policies and programs with the halo of science. They may do this with the best of intentions, or do it even unwittingly. But at the same time, they risk over the long run undermining their own legitimacy -- as all too many have certainly done in the making of energy policy (Baumgartner and Midttun, 1987). Clark and Majone (1984:35) observe a general development along such lines:

> There is still a great respect for learning among politicians and policymakers, but there is also much greater skepticism and suspicion, and the image of objective "value-freek" science and scholarship is severely tarnished (cited from Harvey Brooks). But the unquestioning acceptance of science's legitimacy no longer holds .... What we see then is that the postwar numinous legitimacy of science has been eroded, leaving in its wake a need for a socially negotiated civil legitimacy. Our society's great preoccupation in recent years with "public interest" and "critical" science, with hearing procedures and "independent" assessments, and with demands for "better" ethical standards of scientific practice reflect both the urgency and the difficulty of those negotiations.

Critical examination of science and, in particular, policy research, contributes to making more transparent the political role of scientific elites in modern society. Hopefully, this would increase the level of *self-knowledge and self-discipline within scientific communities*. The role of applied science in policy-making and public debate can and should be more precisely delimited. This could contribute to reducing the abuse of scientific authority in political life. And it would do much to guarantee the continued legitimacy and support of science, including the social sciences, in modern society.

In the following chapters, we suggest a well-defined role for science and expertise in policy-making and politics, a role consistent with democratic politics.

NOTES

[1] This is the *one-dimensional rationality of modern technocracy.* It reduces and distorts the essential complexities of the world and the genuine uncertainty that human existence entails.

[2] We agree with Majone (1986:37) that the scientist or expert engaged in policy-making cannot readily separate the role of expert from that of advocate. Indeed:

> To explain and defend a reasonable course of action under circumstances where the theoretical optimum is unknown or practically unattainable is an essential part of the adviser's job. To draw a sharp line between explanation and advocacy in such cases is next to impossible. It is equally impossible to insulate policy advice from value choices. To quote Walter Heller..., "value judgments are an inescapable, obligatory, and desirable part of the life of an economic adviser." To say anything of importance in the policy process requires value judgments and the willingness to defend those judgments.

But once the political element is integrated into scientific advice, science is no longer pure.

[3] As Gustafsson (1976:15) points out in paraphrasing Weber concerning the social sciences, changing society is the task of the politician, not the social scientist. Gustafsson continues:

In relation to the politician, the social scientist presents an analysis of the problems, indicates alternative courses of action and explains their consequences. But it is not for the social scientist to tell the politicians *which* course to select. That is the politicians' business. The recommendation of a specific course of action presupposes or implies a definite political judgment or standpoint. Naturally, the social scientist himself adopts a certain standpoint and should, in the interest of scientific candour, explain it. But he should not *in his capacity as a social scientist* become an advocate of it. If he does, he abandons his role as a social scientist and himself becomes a politician. Science and politics must be kept separate.

[4] Karpik (1981) refers to logics of social action on the basis of which individuals and groups organize their thinking, decisions, and action. Wittrock (1986) conceives of policy settings as operating according to one or more logics. In the case of multiple logic situations, incompatibilities arise. In this way he conceptualizes *unitary and diverse logic realms of policy-making.* In rule system terms, the different logics of social action are structured and regulated by distinct social rule systems.

[5] The emergence and consolidation of these communities can be historically traced. As Boulding (1964:39) observes:

The foundation of the Royal Society in London in the latter half of the seventeenth century is a crucial date. Here science begins to emerge as an organized subculture. Even then science was still largely a work of amateurs, and the amateur period of science lasted well into the nineteenth century. It is only in the twentieth century that science has become a substantial, organized part of society on a full-time professional basis.

[6] The capability of a scientific community to influence public decision making depends on the specific sociopolitical context in question, the level of consensus and structure of the community, and the power of its theories. These factors contribute to legitimizing the community as "scientific" with the competence, and even the right, to make statements about the area of reality to which science applies.

1. *Theoretical and methodological capabilities.* Some sciences, such as the natural and technical sciences, have considerable explanatory or predictive power, whereas others, such as economics and the social sciences generally, are unable to provide predictions or explanations of the same quality. Of course, that weakness in economics does not prevent economists, in particular, from engaging in the business of making forecasts and predictions, and this much more extensively and with greater authority than their colleagues in the other social sciences. In a certain sense, economists have proved themselves bolder and more adept at exploiting their authority as "genuine scientists." To a considerable degree this has depended on the strength of their profession, a factor to which we now turn.

2. *Professional discipline and authority vis a vis the outside/political world.* Internal professional discipline and closure serve several important structural functions: One function is to to discourage members from making public confessions of the profession's theoretical and methodological failings; Another is to limit public disputes or disagreements among experts of the profes-

sion; (iii) A third is to restrain excessive paradigm cleavages within the profession. Such closing off rests not only on internal professional controls but also on internal discipline vis a vis the larger world.

The case of economics is again an interesting one. Actual predictive power is often low indeed, but the internal discipline of the profession partly compensates for that. Sociology and political science, however, have not apparently managed to discipline their memberships and to ensconce themselves to a comparable degree.

A shared paradigm, even if of low explanatory or predictive power, can play an important role in establishing and maintaining internal discipline. It also may provide the self-confidence to engage publicly in the forecasting business. The possible parallels with the Greek Oracle and with prophets in history would be worth investigating systematically. (We are indebted to Leon Lindberg in suggesting some of these insights.)

[7] We do not assume that the social rule systems of scientific communities are fully consistent and complete. Among other things, there are "contending schools" within any scientific community. Moreover, there are diverse subsets of rules applying to particular settings of scientific activity. For instance, the rules guiding the "context of discovery" or of practical research itself tend to differ from those govering the "context of justification" or the presentation of analyses and results (Reichenbach, 1982).

The internal contradictions and dilemmas arise in part because the institution of science incorporates potentially incompatible norms and values (Merton, 1976). For instance, the value placed upon originality leads scientists to want their priority to be recognized, at the same time that the value set upon humility leads them to insist on how little they have in fact been able to accomplish. Also, Merton identified contradictions between the core norms and values of the discipline and tactical, pragmatic norms having to do with the practical production processes and relationships of power within a discipline. There are also conflicts between sub-communities, schools, and scientific traditions with competing paradigms and methodologies within a scientific community.

[8] (131) Boulding (1964:40) argues that the stability of scientific knowledge depends in part on the fact that inferences of science are drawn not from observation but from theories, thus serving to buffer "the scientific community against the rejection of its inferences or rejection of its messages or observations."

[9] The core rules and procedures of a scientific discipline -- including those of an informal nature learned through practical research experience -- give identity to the scientific enterprise.

[10] As Douglas and Wildavsky (1982:49) note:

> In our modern world people are supposed to live and die subject to known, measurable natural forces, not subject to mysterious moral agencies. That mode of reasoning, indeed, is what makes modern man modern. Science wrought this change between us and nonmoderns. It is hardly true, however, that their universe is more unknown than ours. For anyone disposed to worry about the unknown, science has actually expanded the universe about which we cannot speak with confidence.... This is the double-edged thrust of science, generating new ignorance with new knowledge. The same ability to detect causes and connections or parts per trillion can leave more

unexplained than was left by cruder measuring instruments.

[11] Policy research governed largely by the norms of science would be most likely in instances where: (a) science has a well-established legitimacy in society and the relevant scientific community is strongly cohesive and committed to the integrity of scientific rules; (b) the research community is either largely segregated or buffered from policymakers, their games, and their exercise of power or the policy process itself entails relatively unambiguous problems with minimum controversy (non-partisan). Under such conditions, the products of research would be methodologically governed; they would entail knowledge-based statements or analyses relevant to policy-related phenomena, possibly with an indication of feasible policy alternatives for achieving given goals.

Clark and Majone (1984) argue that meta-criteria or evaluation rules can be found that would allow for a more global and balanced practice of scientific inquiries in policy contexts. They assume, too optimistically in our opinion, that scientists will to a large extent provide the meta-criteria of "adequacy," "effectiveness," "value," and "legitimacy."

In our view, the meta-rules and evaluation criteria are to a large extent negotiable, and the actual results will depend on the arguments and on the authority and power resources that scientific communities can mobilize. In some policy settings their bargaining position may be stronger and more sustained than in others.

[12] Forms of policy research include, among others, different types of reference-group and interactive research, participatory research, and scenario analysis conducted in group and public discussions in which diverse interests are represented.

[13] Coleman (1982:165-66) refers to opposing views on the rationally functioning society:

> L. Haworth develops such a conception and terms it "the experimenting society," seeing it as a desirable model for the future development of society. Jurgen Habermas sees it also as a model for the future development of society, but an oppressive and dangerous one. His objection lies in its bypassing of politics and the clash of interests which make up politics.

[14] In practice, policy-making sometimes functions in this way. Coleman (1982:169-70) observes:

> In a number of cases (research on ... school desegregation, research on school effects, criminological research) the results have been used not by an administrator or by a government agency but by interested parties in the public debate surrounding the policy. In fact, it can be argued that such research has more often been used by outside parties opposed to the policies of an administrative authority, to provide a "window" into an activity that would otherwise be hidden by administrative interests. Research often finds that the effectiveness of a policy does not match the claims for it and thus gives legitimacy to opposition to that policy.... Policy research pluralistically formulated and openly published may strengthen the hand of those interests without administrative authority, by redressing the information imbalance between those in authority and those outside. The dangers of this pluralistic policy research, if any, are to weak-

en central authority vis-a-vis outside interests, not to strengthen it.

This is, indeed, a danger. Government authority is essential
to the implementation of policies and public adherence to
laws and the rules of the game. Processes undermining the
credibility and authority of government -- including those set
in motion by government itself -- can be a serious threat to a
modern, social order.

[15] In this regard, Stern (1987:30) observes:

There is a widely held misconception that
science can establish a single truth on matters related to health risks and that truth
can be communicated by a single source.
This belief is largely responsible for the
confusion many people experience in the
face of scientific conflict, and it needs to be
dispelled. The problem probably reqires a
long-term educational strategy which is not
structural, but which might in time make it
easier to implement the structural solutions.
It is worth considering a change in the way
science is taught in the schools to emphasize that science proceeds not by discoveries
of truths that are immediately recognized as
such, but by a search for truth among competing theories and conflicting evidence.
The implications of that view of science
could be extended to the matter of citizens'
roles when they act politically on matters
involving scientific controversy: people
need to learn to expect conflicting represen-
tations of knowledge when the facts are in
dispute and to search through the conflict
for better understanding. A structural innovation in this spirit would be to prepare a

citizens' guide to the ways risk communicators can slant the facts to favor one side or the other.

4

DEMOCRATIC DISCOURSE, EXPERTISE, AND ALTERNATIVE FUTURES

4.1   THE POINT OF DEPARTURE

Democracy presupposes that citizens and their representatives have the capacity to understand alternatives and to make choices[1]. One of the fundamental methods of democracy is discussion, discussion to enable the formulation of alternatives, increase understanding and faciliate agreement, or at least the making of majority decisions. Majone (1986:2-4) describes the liberal ideal:

> According to classical liberal theory, public discussion of competing ideas and proposals leads to a compromise in which all conflicting opinions are reconciled and which can be accepted by all because it bears the imprint of all. The members of the community participate in public deliberation in order to promote their own views and interests, but in the process they also improve their understanding of the issue under debate and may even be persuaded to change their values and criteria of choice.

> The process of discussion develops sequentially in separate but interconnected forums: in political parties as they formulate their programs and

identify the issues for electoral debate; in the
electorate, as it discusses issues and candidates,
and expresses a majority in favor of one of the
programs; in the legislature, where the majority
attempts to translate the programs into law, in
constant debate with the opposition; in the executive branch, where the discussion of new policies is carried forward to the chief executive and
the cabinet; in the courts, where the adversary
system provides powerful incentives for agencies
and interested parties to present the strongest
arguments in favor of their respective positions.
The entire process is homogenous since it involves debate and persuasion at each stage. But
it is also functionally differentiated since each
organ of public deliberation -- political parties,
electorate, legislature, executive, courts -- has a
specific function in the process. The various or-
gans debate an issue in different form, and from
different points of view, but since they all discuss the same issue, they are all interconnected.
The difference involved is not so much a difference between election, legislation, administration, and adjudication considered as separate
spheres of action: it is the difference between
the electoral, legislative, administrative and judicial form of public deliberation in contributing
to the total solution of the same fundamental issues.

Government by discussion is, in the words of
Walter Bagehot, a plant of singular delicacy. A
method of governance based on the interchange
and mutual criticism of competing ideas and on
the common acceptance of the idea which wins
the competitive struggle, is constantly exposed to
a number of threats. For this reason public de-

liberation has been carefully institutionalized in all modern democracies. This has led to elaborate codes of electoral, parliamentary, administrative, and judicial procedure. For example, electoral laws serve to regularize patterns of citizen input in the policy-making process so as to limit other forms of participation, such as political protest or mass demonstration. Texts like Jefferson's *Manual of Parliamentary Practice* and *Robert's Rules of Order* are the fruit of centuries of experience in coping with the practical problems of public deliberation. The general purpose of procedural rules is to ensure the hearing of every opinion without compromising the need to reach a conclusion. Such is the importance of such rules that *the history of democratic government may be described as the history of the various procedures devised to institutionalized and regulate public deliberation.* (emphasis added) In addition to procedural safeguards, various substantive conditions must also be satisfied. Common deliberation presupposes some common ground; without shared values and understandings discussion quickly degenerates in unending dispute. Some measure of social equality and reasonably equal access to information is also highly desirable, since the ideal discussion is that among equals. But the most basic prerequisite of public deliberation is that the members of the community agree to focus the debate on some issues of general interest. Before the dialectic of conflicting positions can unfold, there must be widespread agreement about the nature of the central problems facing the community at a given time.

Many of our contemporary forms of public deliberation, assembly, representation, and decision making are extensions and elaborations of classical Greek and Roman forms. To a large extent they are unsuitable for dealing with many of the complex problems of the modern world, particularly problems associated with the development of high science and technology. The basic constitutional arrangements of many nations -- and their corresponding "theories of democracy" -- were established long before the problems of large-scale complex industrial societies presented themselves (Dahl, 1982). Modern democracies are faced with decisions about radically new technological developments, which unfold in a fraction of the time earlier technological developments took. The decisions concern not only new sociotechnical systems but new social relationships and conditions, such as linkages between large groups of experts and democratically elected policymakers. They also concern the future development of work and leisure, or even the survival of humankind.

Several of the questions which we wish to address in this and the following chapter are as follows:

What kind of science and expertise does democratic politics need in order to realize its spirit? In what ways can democratic steering and consensus formation be organized and carried out in a world of expertise, where the principles of technocracy tend to prevail?

And what kind of politics does science need in order to contribute to informed and reliable decisions in shaping human conditions?

In addressing these questions, we have felt it essential to begin with certain fundamentals: the nature of democratic discourse and decision making and the possible roles experts should play in this process. Our challenge, as we came to understand it, has been to formulate institutional principles for organized democratic discourse and decision making in a world of elaborate expertise, large-scale technology, and organized science[2]. This is also a world in which bureaucratic and non-democratic forms are widespread and seem particularly suitable for mobilizing and using expert knowledge. This is often done at the expense of the democratic process. In general, contemporary forms of democratic action -- which Western societies have inherited from the past, reforming and developing them in the course of history and political struggle -- have proved inadeqate in two fundamental ways:

- The authority and legitimacy of democratic decision are often rendered marginalized by decision making dominated by experts working hand in hand with bureaucratic power. At the same time, the norms and integrity of systematic knowledge, including science, are frequently subverted or compromised by the policy process. This increases the likelihood of misinformed or biased policy-making and government action, at least action uninformed by many important social values and public concerns, which designers and planners of large-scale sociotechnical systems are prone to ignore or slight.

- Conventional democratic institutions, political rules of the game, and prevailing political styles are largely incapable of dealing systematically with the issues and problems associated with many contemporary scientific and technological developments.

The rights to freedom of speech and to influence over one's conditions implies the capability to exercise such rights. In other words, *citizens and their representatives are expected to have the capacity to formulate an informed concept or opinion. Freedom of expression -- or possession of a point of view -- is*

meaningless with regard to technical and scientific areas unless one has the *expertise, or access to it, to formulate a point
of view.*

Today, much of the capacity to work out concepts or
designs for the future lies in the hands of major enterprises
and some public agencies, including the military, and with
the technicians and expert groups that serve or work closely
with these organizations. They invest in and support scientific and technological developments implied by their particular interests and conceptions of sociotechnical reality. Politicians and citizens lacking that capacity are to a large extent
unable to articulate an intelligent point of view concerning
sociotechnical questions and futures. They remain, therefore, largely helpless in the face of revolutionary technological developments.

These failures are the backdrop for the formulation in
the following sections of new strategies for organizing the
democratic process in the context of modern science and
technology.

4.2 SOME PRINCIPLES FOR SYSTEMATIC DEMOCRATIC DISCOURSE

We begin with a generalized concept of democracy, namely,
a culture of norms and values and social relations in which
societal actors -- policymakers, political representatives, ne-
gotiators, citizens -- are expected to treat one another as
equals and engage in discourse and negotiation with one another, concerning public decisions and societal regulation[3].

Any concrete institution of democracy consists of a set
of more or less shared principles and rules. These specify --
and provide a frame for -- the organizatin of group or collective discussion and decision making (Burns et al, 1985; Burns
and Flam, 1987). In general, the rules specify (cf. Frohlich
and Oppenheimer, 1978):

- The classes of legitimate issues or problems that are discussable and subject to decision.

- The participants included (and explicitly or implicitly, those excluded) and their different roles.

- The procedures and legitimate resources to be used in conducting discussions and group decision making.

- The distribution of resources (votes) among participants and the value assigned to different resources.

- The procedures whereby votes (or resources assigned value) are to be aggregated to yield a collective choice.

- The acceptable or legitimate options that may be brought up for discussion and collective decision.

We shall briefly expand on a couple of these points in order to specify further the actors, issues, and forms for democratic discourse.

Issues or Problems

Politics always begins with the second position, an alternative, and the question of how to deal with two or more alternatives. The setting may be one of policy-making, legislation, mobilization and allocation of resources, imposition of burdens, opportunities for gain, or redistribution of resources. In general, policy and program alternatives may be formulated, and choices have to be made. Legal requirements may call for a decision. Or political agents may advance contradictory proposals for policies or policy instruments, the mobilization and use of resources, or the distribution of resources.

The alternative proposals, courses of action, and ultimate aims often appear mutually exclusive in terms of resource requirements or the practicalities of implementation. We are concerned, above all, with *alternative sociotechnical futures or systemic alternatives.* This matter entails consideration of, for instance, different systems of energy production and consumption, transportation, defense, health care, work organization, and so forth. Such considerations are very different undertakings from those involving piecemeal adjustments or alterations of parameters *within an established system.*

Several of the factors that give rise to alternative approaches or strategies, that is, systemic alternatives, are:

1. *Conflicting values or goals.* One group or agent values the commercial exploitation and use of a resource -- for example, land, water, forests -- while another values maximizing the preservation of these resources in their natural state.

2. *Scarce resources.* The resources available are insufficient to launch and develop more than one of the systemic alternatives, and the actors involved disagree, for instance, about the efficacy or performance capabilities of alternative systems: nuclear power as opposed to renewable energy systems or radical energy conservation programs.

3. *Alternative regimes.* The organizing principles and institutional arrangements to which the interested parties are committed are: private versus public medical systems with highly advanced, costly technologies; centralized versus decentralized administration of social services; commercial versus non-commercial organization of educational and recreational facilities.

The agents involved may disagree about the apparent efficiency of the systemic alternatives, degree of irreversibility, or distributional consequences (that is, capacity to generate very substantial disparities in life chances). In these cases, the agents need not necessarily disagree generally on ideology or values concerning alternative institutional arrangements.

In some cases, systemic alternatives reflect the *one-dimensional perspectives of their advocates.* Many technological policy and political-technological discussions and proposals are formulated in terms of a single issue, measure, or project (a single dimension or very few dimensions) without sufficiently taking into account the larger framework and context of the issue. Systematic democratic discourse is designed to broaden the perspectives of the actors involved -- and to unleash creative potentials to discover or to develop new alternatives. In our view, there can be only the most limited mutual understanding between political agents advocating systemic alternatives if they fail to grasp the underlying complex set of values and assumptions, factual assertions, inferences, and arguments that constitute their alternative proposals.

Deciding Participants

The deciding participants are "voters," political leaders or representatives, "policymakers.'[4]' They consider issues, alternatives, or decisions. Their choices make a difference, and in this sense they exercise social power.

The social agents involved may compose a committee, council, assembly, or an electorate. They may be individual voters, caucuses, blocs, parties, other organizations, or nations. The essential condition is that the *participants are more or less equal and have the power to discuss and to make choices -- including the veto power to* block choices -- and the choice enacted makes a *difference, that is, determines to a greater or lesser extent a* result[5].

As a general principle, actors or groups of actors affected by the issue or decision in question -- now or in the future -- should participate or be duly represented. No relevant, that is "affected," agent should be excluded. However, any actor, or the groups and organizations which they represent, that refuses to accept or abide by the core organizing principles and norms of democratic discourse should be subject to exclusion. This is a normative minimum required of every participant. The principle is essential in order to sustaining democratic forms over time and across generations. Thus, violence is excluded from a genuine democracy except for the minimum violence -- or threat of violence -- utilized to enforce basic principles and to exclude persons or groups that would seek to destroy or refuse to abide by the basic principles. However, even here exclusion should be used with great care and always with due process supervised and protected by independent courts.

Democratic Process

Modern democratic theory -- and to a great extent the prevailing ideology -- stresses decision procedures, voting, votes of the participants. In our view, *insufficient attention is given to discourse, social learning, and consensus formation.* Of course, the important role of decision rules and procedures and their impact on final outcomes must be duly recognized. The choice of rules and procedures for aggregating votes and reaching collective decisions makes a difference, substantial in some cases (Nurmi, 1984): plurality, majority, and unanimity rules; rules allowing or excluding voting on one, two, or more alternatives at a time, among others. Here, however, we want to focus on the *social organization of systematic democratic discourse,* since this aspect of democratic practice is essential, in our view, to addressing major questions of modern science and technology.

Majone (1986:38) observes that the challenge of developing public discourse and the use of reason in such discourse, have been major concerns of political philosophy since antiquity:

Building on the practice of government by discussion in the city state, the Greeks developed a general technique of public discourse which they called dialectic. This is a method of argumentation characterized not so much by the form of reasoning (discussion by question and answers came to be regarded as its paradigmatic form) as by the nature of its premises and the social context of its applications.... The starting point of a dialectic argument are not more or less arbitrary assumptions, but points of view already present in the community; its conclusion is not a formal proof *but shared understanding of an issue.* While scientific disciplines are specialized forms of knowledge, available only to the experts, dialectic is not confined to any special science and can be used by everbody since, as Aristotle writes, we all have occasion to criticize or defend an argument, to defend ourselves or to accuse.

For the Greeks dialectical reasoning had three main uses. First, as a method of critical inquiry into the foundations and assumptions of the different specialized sciences (or perspectives). Second, as a technique for arguing in favor of one's own viewpoint and a procedure for clarifying controversial issues since "if we are able to raise difficulties on both sides, we shall more easily discern both truth and falsehood on every point." Finally, and most important, dialectic was conceived of as an educational process that transforms the common man into an informed citizen and the specialist into a person able to communicate with his or her fellow citizens. Criticism, advocacy of new ideas and education remain to this day the most important contributions that policy analysts and advisors can make to the process of democratic policy making.

Democratic discussion and decision making entail social exchange, negotiation, and collective policy-making[6]. There are rules and procedures for organizing discussion, procedures for articulating alternatives, and various strategies for reaching compromises. The purpose of organized democratic discourse, as we have envisioned it, is to reach understandings and agreements on one or more courses of action: to establish or not to establish a large-scale sociotechnical system; to devolve or to continue an existing system.

In democratic discourse, political agents -- groups, organizations, and parties -- formulate alternative designs for sociotechnical systems or futures. These entail different approaches or institutional strategies to tackle the problem or to realize the purposes for which a proposed technology or sociotechnical system is designed. Examples of sociotechnical alternatives have been mentioned earlier: nuclear energy versus non-nuclear energy systems, private versus public telecommunication systems or transport systems, pharmaceutical research and development and therapy versus preventive and natural health infrastructures. The conceptualization of such systemic alternatives feeds into the processes of discourse, articulation, and reformulation, furthering dialogue and negotiation among agents.

Politics and Expertise

In a world of high science and technology, politics and expertise should be brought together in ways that allow politics to articulate, develop, and choose among alternative positions. At the same time experts advise and contribute to the systematic articulation and analysis of alternatives. Purely political considerations, particularly in highly technical areas, are likely to lead to disaster[7]. Nevertheless, purely technical decisions may mask value positions and important issues. Sooner or later such positions and issues are likely to lead to societal tensions and conflicts and to increased economic and political costs. The latter can be minimized, or in some instances avoided altogether, if political differences and problems are explicitly dealt with at the start.

In this regard Douglas and Wildavsky (1982:49, 63-64) point out:

> Experts are used to disagreement. But they are *not used to failing to understand why they disagree.*... Scientists disagree on whether there are problems, what solutions to propose, and if intervention will make things better or worse. One scientist thinks of Mother Nature as merely secreting a healthy amount of dirt and another thinks of her being forced to ingest lethal pollutants. No wonder the ordinary lay person has difficulty in follówng the argument, and no wonder the scientists have difficulty presenting themselves in public.

> If the lack of agreement among scientists is due to absence of knowledge, (then) as information increases, disputes would decrease. On the other hand, better measurement opens more possibilities, more research brings more ignorance to the light of day. The tendency toward confrontation instead of disputation may be due to the kind of questions asked, questions that do not permit of widely acceptable answers. If the questions are about how much risk is acceptable, *social as well as scientific answers are required.* (Emphasis added)

The political agents or policymakers carry on discourse, negotiate, and make collective decisions in democratic ways. These processes involve experts. Their involvement facilitates the systematic introduction of technical knowledge and arguments into the discussion and decision making. Technical experts and scientists assist the political agents involved in formulating their systemic alernatives, articulating specific ways in which such systems could be established, financed, organized, and operated. They also contribute to the analysis of possible as well as likely consequences of each sociotechnical proposal. Through institutionalized processes of formulating, examining, and discussing *alternative systems and futures,* a mechanism is provided for regulating technical and scientific claims. Equally as important, politics itself is subject to the discipline of systematic knowledge.

The open politics of formulating and choosing alternative future developments, where political agents clearly play out their value-bearing and decision-making roles, is intended to help maintain the integrity of expert or scientific knowledge. However, experts in their professional roles are not expected to determine the choice between options based on different value orientations and visions of society. That is the task or role of the citizenry or their representatives.

4.3   THE PHASES AND ORGANIZATION OF DEMOCRATIC DISCOURSE: A MODEL

The model of democratic discourse and negotiation outlined below entails both new and old methods, procedures, and forms of social organization. These may be activated or introduced and developed in a committee, commission of enquiry, assembly, or other collectivity. The organizing principle and procedures making up the social form are designed:

- To link systematically as well as to regulate the interplay of politics and expert knowledge so as to maintain the integrity and vitality of politics and human values, on the one hand, and expert knowledge, on the other;

- To generate and develop systematically a set of alternatives for democratic discourse and decision making;

- To allow more comprehensive descriptions and presentations of alternatives for future action and development;

- To enable an investigation and analysis of the preconditions and consequences of the alternatives;

- To facilitate discourse and negotiation among social agents concerning different alternatives for future action and development;

- To open up political deliberation to consideration of new values and action possibilities, intelligent reassessments, and value shifts. *Thus, a more systematic basis for social learning and consensus formation may be realized.* New sociotechnical alternatives, which possibly transcend different perspectives and conflicts, may be identified and developed.

In organized democratic discourse, at least three types of participants or roles can be distinguished: (a) participants who are to discuss and negotiate collective decisions; (b) experts who provide information and analyses to the participants, either to the entire collectivity or to specific groups of participants who formulate systemic alternatives; and (c) moderators or mediators (in some cases these may be the participants themselves playing such a role in relation to themselves). The latter are particularly important where parties with intense conflict or opposition participate. A third party may have the responsibility not only to assure adherence to the rules and procedures of discourse and negotiation but to assist the participants in searching for and exploring new or alternative options, particularly options that might be mutually acceptable.

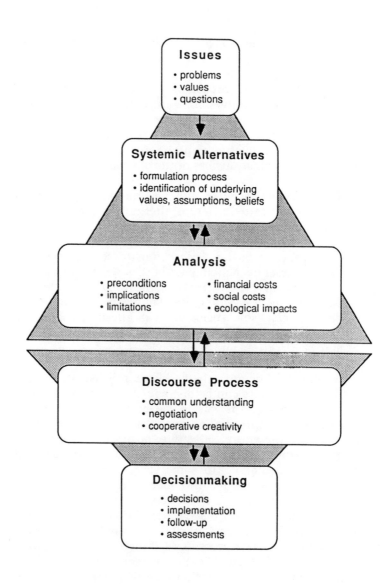

Figure 4.1   Democratic Discourse and Decision Making

Democratic discourse and negotiation have five phases, plus an implementation phase (see Figure 4.1). The phases are briefly discussed below. We stress that this is a general design. In concrete instances, the general design is filled in and elaborated, taking into account situational conditions, the specific actors involved, their established or historical relationships and predispositions, and the issues at stake.

Phase I. Issue Identification

> Among participating agents and groups, identify issues relating to a proposed or existing technology or sociotechnical system. This may concern, for example, nuclear energy, genetic engineering, tele-communications, and the U.S. Strategic Defense Initiative (SDI or Star Wars). Discourse already begins in this phase, as the actors involved raise questions and identify problems or issues they consider should be discussed and decided.

Phase IIA. Formulation of Systemic Alternatives

> In this phase, formulate or reconstruct systemic alternatives, that entail different approaches to or strategies for dealing with the problems or goals for which a proposed technology or sociotechnical system is designed. An alternative proposal may have already been formulated prior to or in connection with Phase I. In that case, an essential task in Phase II is to articulate and systematize *at least one alternative* to the initial or main proposal. The alternatives may entail more or less functionally equivalent ways to realize the same goal, but with very different preconditions and consequences. Examples of such

sociotechnical alternatives are nuclear energy versus solar systems, private car transport systems versus public transport systems (or mixed systems), private versus public health care systems, alternative systems for utilizing computers and information technologies in factories and offices, alternative defense systems.

Scientists and other technical experts play an important role in assisting the social actors involved *to formulate and articulate their systemic alternatives*. This concerns, in particular, identification of ways in which such options could or should be organized, financed, and operated.

The alternatives that are formulated, examined, and compared should be presented in ways the participants holding different perspectives can accept. The advocates of each systemic alternative should have access to expertise they trust, either either because it is genuinely neutral and professional or because it is loyal to their option. The systemic alternatives that are suggested or advocated by political agents become foci in the processes of discourse, further elaboration, reformulation, and negotiation among the participants.

Phase IIB. Identification of Underlying Values and Purposes

Identify the basic purposes and values which underlie systemic alternatives. This entails investigating the value implications or value constellations inherent in systemic alternatives.

The identification phase serves to expose underlying consensus or cleavage. It lays bare actors' different cognitive, value, or existential perspectives. It enables the participants to recognize and to understand alternative technological futures that arise because of the participants' differing values, normative concepts, and underlying assumptions. This would concern, for instance, nuclear power as opposed to a program of radical energy savings, a public transport system as opposed to one based largely on private transportation with automobiles, pharmaceutical research and development versus development of natural health measures, alternative systems for designing and developing computerized offices and factories.

Phase III. Limitation and Impact Analyses

Specify and analyze the implications and limits of the systemic alternatives in terms of knowledge obtained from phase II. This entails also exposing, often through sustained discourse, the areas of uncertainty each and every systemic alternative or plan entails. Competing alternatives have their unique uncertainties and vulnerabilities. Exposing and examining these can open the way for compromises and alternative proposals that transcend the initial proposals.

Here, as in phase IIA, experts and scientists play important roles. In this phase they specify the feasibility and impacts of the systemic alternatives under consideration. Thus, the economic, technical, legal, or social consequences, for instance, of a nuclear future as opposed to a solar future would be examined. Existing methods and analytical tools, such as technology assessment and scenario analysis, can be usefully brought to bear in this phase of the process[8].

In this regard, Dietz (1987: 60) has recently advocated the use of social impact assessment methods and techniques in facilitating public discussion and learning:

Social impact assessment can translate all policy consequences into social consequences which are comprehensible and salient to the public. A rancher might not understand nor care much about the cost-effectiveness of a particular public lands policy. But he or she will understand and be concerned with the impact of a policy on his or her ranch, neighbors, and town. An Ohio steelworker won't care about or understand a loss of plant (botanical) diversity in a section of range, but he or she may be concerned about a reduction in sightseeing or hunting opportunities. Broadening and deepening public interest and understanding can also depolarize debate. If a rancher's only source of information about a policy is the Cattlemen's Association, he or she will think only about the economics of the plan. If a Social Impact Assessment points out the consequences of alternative policies for ranch economics, hunting opportunities, and local service costs, the rancher will have a better view of the tradeoffs inherent in any decision and will be less inclined to support all or nothing positions....

A policy may preserve a Native American burial ground but hurt the income of the timber industry. Another policy may destroy the burial ground but improve timber production. If each set of impacts is clearly portrayed, when a particular policy is chosen, it is obvious (when) the resource manager has valued the cultural resources over the economic productivity or vice versa. Social Impact Assessment does not indicate which decision is best, but it does differentiate scientific or factual information from values or political judgments.

In sum, technical and scientific knowledge inputs play an essential role in analyses of constraints and impacts and the search for feasible, broadly acceptable solutions. Such considerations indicate what cannot be done or which policies or programs would entail great costs or risks. Majone (1986:11-12) has pointed out that an important part of the job of policy analysts is to improve the quality of public debate by helping policy makers and the general public avoid both reckless underestimation and harsh overstatement of the possible. Feasibility analysis identifies the major actual or potential constraints (without ignoring political and administrative feasibility). These are distinguished from fictitious obstacles. The constraints are evaluated in terms of their significance for different implementation strategies. Estimates are made of the costs and benefits of relaxing those constraints not absolutely fixed (Majone, 1986:12)[9].

Phase IVA. Engagement in Discourse Proper

Initiate organized discourse between actors or groups advocating different systemic alternatives. The guiding questions here are, What should we do? For what purposes? How should we do it? With what resources and means? Who should do it? When? Where? The process is intended to maximize the production and exchange of information not only in order to explore or to expose limitations and disadvantages in each alternative, but also to learn about opportunities and advantages of different alternatives and the possibilities of achieving realistic compromises or generating entirely new alternatives that incorporate or transcend initial alternatives.

The discourse process contributes to the expansion of collective knowledge, increasing the likelihood of achieving new insights into or conceptions of the possible. Underlying tensions and conflicts also tend to be exposed. Without suppressing differences or conflicts, the discourse process contributes to the formation of a more holistic or global perspective, opening up possibilities of discovering or identifying innovative, even transcendant alternatives. This is essential to creative politics. Majone argues (1986:19-20):

> Assessing policy feasibility is only one aspect of a continuous process of evaluation in which all members of a democratic community are engaged. Citizens, legislators, administrators, judges, experts, the media -- all contribute their particular perspectives and evaluative criteria. This multiplicity of viewpoints is not only unavoidable in a pluralistic society but also necessary to the vitality of a system of government by discussion. Nevertheless, as Northrop Frye has remarked in the context of literary criticism, there seems to be no reason why the larger understanding of public policy to which these separate perspectives are contributing should remain forever invisible to them, as the coral atoll to the polyp.

Democratic discourse -- by systematically exposing different perspectives on technological development to one another through the discourse process -- encourages a level of understanding and appreciation that is more than the sum of the separate evaluations (Majone, 1986:20). As Majone stresses (1986:20):

> The purpose is not to construct a grand model that would combine all the partial perspectives into one general criterion of good policy -- a weighted combination, so to speak, of equity, efficiency, effectiveness, legality, legitimacy, and any other relevant standard -- but to contribute to a shared understanding of the multiple perspectives involved.

Understanding is, above all, a process more than a final state.

Phase IVB. Reiteration and Reformulation

> Phases I-IVA are reiterated in the course of discussion and negotiation. Social learning and reassessment processes may lead not only to refinements but to reconceptualization. Also, new systematic alternatives, incorporating or transcending those initially under consideration, may be introduced into the discussion and developed in the reiterative and reflective processes.

Phase V. Making Decisions Socially

> This phases entails the activiation and implementation of formal and informal rules and procedures for negotiating and reaching a collective decision.

In some cases, a high degree of consensus is required in order to mobilize resources or to bring about essential technical, economic, political, and legal changes connected with major technological innovations and developments (see later discussion). Such circumstances often provide incentives for reaching an agreement, for instance, by finding alternatives that transcend those initially considered and that are acceptable to the parties involved. Compromise and transcendance are the arts of politics, which organized democratic discourse is designed to facilitate.

Phase VI. Implementation

Economic resources, people, and authority are mobilized to implement the decision. Social learning through doing and through assessment of real impacts and developments often leads to reiteration of the entire process at later points in time. It is essential that the implementation of one or more systemic alternatives be followed up with systematic data collection, impact studies, periodic assessments, and review in order to facilitate social learning and development. In this way a knowledge base is provided for future re-assessments and collective decision making.

Our proposal concerns, then, organizing sustained democratic discourse in order to enable the formulation, development, and assessment of alternative sociotechnical systems or futures. Such democratic discourse allows -- even calls for -- the interaction of political agents and technical-scientific expertise. However, it specifies relatively well-defined roles in doing so. *By insisting on generating alternative proposals in a systematic way, a mechanism is provided for regulating technical and scientific claims. At the same time, political values and ambitions can be subject to the discipline of expert knowledge.*

The discourse process serves at least three purposes:

- *It helps increase awareness among participants that there are possible alternatives to any given technology or sociotechnical system,* for example, energy systems or systems of telecommunications;

- *It helps provide insights into the deep structure of systemic alternatives:* the differing fundamental values, norms, assumptions, models of human behavior, models of social relationships and the desirable organization of society, and models of relations between society and nature. Each participant is exposed to his or her own assumptions and values as well as those of others. Participants are challenged to recognize and understand their agreements and differences at more profound levels than in conventional politcal exchange. No book or library can provide such an education[10].

- *It increases the probability of reaching consensus based on argumentation and persuasion, in part through* appeals to norms and values, application of expert knowledge, and the formulation of additional alternatives. Thus, new alternatives may be articulated or created which take better account of the multiple perspectives and values articulated in the discourse.

Organized democratic discourse entails, hence, a social form designed to strongly couple politics and the knowledge of experts in such a way as to maintain the integrity of politics, on the one hand, and that of expert knowledge, on the other[11].

114

4.4   CONCLUSION

We are proposing that democratic discourse, organized in the manner outlined in this chapter, can and should be carried out in a variety of settings in which major technological developments and their impacts are issues or should be issues: parliamentary bodies; special hearings, commissions, and government agencies; labor-management forums; universities and research institutes (see next chapter on systematic democratic discourse)[12]. Such organized discourse not only would address issues of technological development and applications of science but would facilitate a partial shift from competitive or adversary politics to more open, creative politics. This is, in our view, an essential transition if modern democratic societies are to deal effectively with high science and technology and, indeed, if human societies are to survive over the long run.

The concept of systematic democratic discourse is an open, reflective one. Democratic discourse should expose and articulate assumptions and the models of different systemic alternatives that underlie, for instance, energy systems, automobile transportation systems, major industrial facilities, strategies to deal with pollution, genetic engineering developments, telecommunication systems, and national defense alternatives. Methods and strategies can be developed to assist participants to articulate, elaborate, and to reflect on their alternative perspectives. In that way, the actors involved can come to both question and understand one another, without insisting that each one agree with the other's perspectives.

Argument and persuasion are part and parcel of such types of discourse. Majone (1986:31) writes:

(I)n politics, unlike in the market, decisions must always be justified. However whimsically policy actors come to their conclusions, plausible arguments for their choices must always be given if they are to be taken seriously in the forums of public deliberation. Advocates of a particular policy must make an argument to convince people who have different views, or no views at all. The argument may be good or bad, simple or sophisticated, but it must be persuasive.

To be persuasive the advocate must give reasons why his or her preferred policy will also be in the general interest, or at least in the interest of others whose support is needed. Now these reasons may be quite different from those that led the advocate to the adoption of the policy in the first place. Hence persuasive arguments of this sort are often dismissed as "rationalizations" -- attempts to justify *a posteriori* one's actions by means of rational reasons rather than by the "real" motives.

But it is not necessarily dishonest or merely "rationalizing" to justify or explain a decision and persuade other people to accept it by giving reasons different from those that actually led to the decision. Policy arguments are not formal proofs. A logical or mathematical proof is either true or false; if it is true, then it automatically wins the assent of any person able to understand it. Arguments are only more or less plausible, more or less convincing to a particular audience. Moreover, there is no unique way to construct an argument: data and evidence can be selected in a wide variety of ways from available information, and there are several alternative methods of analysis and ways of ordering values. Hence, there is nothing intrinsically reprehensible in selecting the particular combination of data, facts, values and analytic methods which seem to be most appropriate to convince a given audience.

A major aim of organized democratic discourse is to faciliate fruitful discussion and effective negotiation, increasing the likelihood of "creative politics." Creative politics makes possible the generation of innovative alternatives and imagining the unimaginable. Democratic discourse -- and processes of argumentation and persuasion -- can contribute in systematic ways to collective learning and consensus formation in the face of the challenges of modern science and technology[13].

NOTES

[1] This presumption is increasingly difficult to maintain
in the modern world. There are several reasons for this
difficulty. (We are particularly grateful to James Douglas for pointing out the following developments, which
suggest a much deeper and more serious challenge to
democracy than that considered in this book in the area
of technology and high science):

- The field of government, and hence the issues to
  be included in democratic discourse, have enor-
  mously expanded. For example, a hundred years
  ago, none or very few would have thought that the
  govenment had more responsibility for controlling
  the economy than for controlling the weather.
  (Imagine the political issues and social conflicts if
  in a hundred years time, governments acquire the
  power to control the weather.) Nineteenth entury
  democratic discourse covered a relatively narrow
  field comprising primarily but not exclusively
  taxation and government finance, law-and-order
  issues, and foreign policy.

- Scientific and technological developments have
  acquired a vastly increased societal impact. In Is-
  aac Newton's day, politicians did not need to wor-
  ry unduly about the effects on foreign policy of
  the law of gravity; or in Benjamin Franklin's day,
  of the theory of electricity. Not so with regard to
  the knowledge of physics, which made possible
  the development of nuclear weapons and nuclear

power or the development of lasers.

- Even within the narrower fields of policy-relevant disciplines, the information explosion is so great that no one person can encompass them all.

- Finally, the number of people requiring the capacity to understand what is going on and what the alternatives are has vastly increased. Early 19th century democratic discourse took place among a restricted group of people in Britain, the United States, and such other countries as had adopted democracy by then. The franchise was restricted by all sorts of property, educational and other qualifications until the last quarter of the century. Women (more than half the present electorate) did not obtain the right to vote until after World War I.

[2] We would agree with Habermas that one notion of a rational organization of society is that "based on a free agreement among its members, is... in however distorted a form... already embodied and recognized in the democratic institutions, the legitimation principles and the self-interpretations of modern industrial societies" (Wellmer, 1985:52). Wellmer adds, however: "Habermas does not try to answer the question *how such institutional structures would look in a post-capitalist society.* This is quite consistent with his general position; it is not the task of the theoretician to determine what the content of a future social consensus will be."

In our view, democratic discourse as a type of "non-distorted, reciprocal communication" cannot be established and maintained unless we conceptualize and institute the social conditions, including the institutional forms for mutual communication (see also Bernstein, 1985:11). Elster (1986:117), in discussing Habermas' theory of politics, stresses the importance of taking the question of institutional and constitutional design very seriously.

We have envisioned our task, at least in part, as precisely one of proposing alternative social forms that could organize more effective democratic processes. Such proposals should be based in part on systematic knowledge of social organization and collective decision-making processes (Burns and Flam, 1987).

[3] There is a great spectrum of notions covered by the term "democracy" (see Dahl, 1976).

Frohlich and Oppenheimer (1978:95) limit the concept of democracy to a set of *decision rules*. They do not require that each individual has equal votes. Nor do they require that all individuals be given the vote. In their view, every voter must be potentially important but not all individuals need be voters. That is, they define democracy independent of notions of (a) universal suffrage or of (b) one person-one vote. Finally, they do not restrict the definition to binary procedures, that is, decisions that are two-way motions or races.

Our approach is to focus on a larger "core," encompassing discourse and negotiation as well as collective decision making. We articulate and develop one set of possible forms.

[4] Thus, the concept of democratic organization encompasses both direct and representative democacy. In the latter case citizens, or "members," freely select representatives, who then participate in collective policy-making and government decisions. In both direct and representative democracy, the judgments of individual agents are combined to reach collective decisions (Frohlich and Oppenheimer, 1978).

In addition to the full participants, there are advisers, consultants, and experts who assist in the formulation, reformulation, and development of alternatives. Also, there is typically a moderator, presiding officer, or mediator. Such roles are discussed briefly later.

[5] Habermas's concept of communicative action, which presupposes non-coercive and non-distortive argumentation, suggests democratic discourse. We differ from Habermas in that we do not consider such a principle inherent or built into everyday, pre-theoretical communication.

Systematic democratic discourse is a social form designed to facilitate public debate of certain issues, negotiation and decision making. *It is purposeful, whereas Habermas's concept of communicative action is not purposeful in this sense.*

We want to stress the importance of purposful discourse. Political questions relating to technological revolution and sociotechnical futures are not simple matters of intellectual discussion, but substantive decision making and are to that extent instrumental (Elster, 1986). Failure to insist on this allows potentially profound discussions to be isolated from mainstream political decision making. The discourse process serves "safety-valve" and symbolic political functions. Such forms contribute to reinforcement of undemocratic decision making, since they divert attention and movement from mainstream policy-making to powerless "discourse" in which "democratic" games are played without substantial import. (See later discussion).

[6] van Gunsteren and Lock (1977) observe:

> An old ideal of political theory is a community of free citizens who settle their common affairs through negotiation and debate. In such a society, it is supposed that people

know each other and have the opportunity to talk to each other. Evidently, this is not possible in a mass society. Many thousands of people cannot talk to each other, let alone conduct a national debate. An application of the concepts and insights from the old political theory, which were based on a situation in which a few citizens were familiar with each other and communicated, is bound to give trouble in the new situation shaped by mass society.

It is obviously not possible to realize small-community democracy in dealing with global (regional or national) problems. Nevertheless, as we argue later, one can organize strategic discourse and negotiation processes, which involve high levels of participation. For instance, this was achieved in the course of the referendum and prior debate in Sweden concerning the future of nuclear power.

[7] The close coupling of politics and expertise in democratic discourse serves, in part, to induce politicians to be more serious and professional about the problems confronting them, in the face of tremendous institutional pressures to engage in ambiguities, avoidance tactics, and platitudes. As we stressed in Chapter 1, political expediency and Machiavellian strategies are commonplace, and, in part, this is a result of the "rules of the game" and the manner in which modern politics is organized.

[8] The concept of "technology assessment" (TA) originiated in the United States in the mid-1960s. It entailed an attempt to develop methods and analytical tools to anticipate or measure the impact of technology (such as studies on risks, markets, and profitability). It was also intended to improve the quality of advice to policymakers. This development should be seen against the back-

drop of the increasing concerns about technological development and the significance of science:

- The increasing social and environmental costs connected with the adoption and development of many modern technologies

- The growth in critical awareness among scientists and the public concerning technical and scientific "progress."

The U.S. Congress established an Office of Technology Assessment (OTA), which began to function in 1973. Its task consisted in supplying Congress with application-oriented information and options with respect to the ecological, economic, social, and political consequences of technical projects and developments. A number of other countries have followed suit. In West Germany in 1986, a Parliamentary Commission responsible for considering the establishment of a TA agency under Parliament proposed setting up such an institution. One of us, Ueberhorst, was a member of this commission.

Many of the techniques and methods of technology assessment created to analyze technological development and its impacts are largely technocratic in character. They are largely designed to ignore or avoid conflicts and, indeed, work relatively well if there are no basic conflicts or if those who might oppose a development are disarmed by expert authority or are unaware of the connection between the development and their own values.

Similarly, much of the work with systems theory and cybernetics has conceptualized processes as problems of system design and management. Generally lacking has been any developed *political concept,* opposing values and interests, conflicts and power struggles, and alternative system designs that would reflect opposition among groups with conflicting values and interests. Etzioni (1968) proposed one approach to developing a much broader conception of systems and cybernetics in his active society and in his exploration of new strategies for consensus building in technically advanced, complex societies. Also see Baumgartner et al (1986).

[9] Majone (1986:13) distinguishes between objective constraints, which are imposed, and policy constraints, which are self-imposed or are the result of prior decisions or methodological choices. He adds (13-14):

> For practical purposes self-imposed limitations may be categorized as follows:
>
> (a) Constraints that are adopted only for a limited purpose or time (e.g., heuristic constraints, temporary standards, conventional definitions of special terms, and so on).
>
> (b) Constraints that are accepted "until further notice" because they are considered important or useful (standard operating procedures, organizational charts, classification schemes such as those used by most administrative agencies, strategic commitments by which one binds oneself in order to gain bargaining advantages in continuous negotiations).
>
> (c) Constraints that are considered, often as a matter of practical experience, to be indispensable for the achievement of certain policy goals (distributional constraints and other equity requirements; rules of reciprocity; "due process;" precedents and conventions).

(d) Constraints that are accepted implicitly, but whose existence is acknowledged only when they are challenged or violated (ethical and cultural norms, behavioral expectations, professional standards, but also preselection biases in problem formulation).

[10] Howard (1982:169) suggests, in discussing Paul Ricoeur's critique of Habermas, that Habermas falls into the error of identifying the problem of understanding with the more narrow problem of understanding another person or actor:

(T)hat is, another's perhaps domineering or exploitative intention, subjectivity, mind -- whether that other be an individual or an institution. He thinks, in too exclusive a sense, that the meaning of a transmissin must be the meaning that other subjects have put there. As long as he thinks this, he will never succeed in escaping subjective -- that is, uncritical assessments of truth.

[11] On a concrete, practical level, this corresponds to Habermas's idea of integrating different types of knowledge. Habermas (1984) suggests that different forms of "rationalities" should come into contact with one another in such a way as to avoid isolating the inner logic of the forms of argumentation specialized in truth, normative correctness, or aesthetic harmony. Jay (1985:133) notes:

Habermas claims that all three spheres of specialized knowledge (cognitive-instrumental, moral-practical, and aesthetic-expressive) would have to be made accessible at once. A reified everyday praxis can be

cured only by creating unconstrained interaction of the cognitive with the moral-practical and the aesthetic-expressive elements.

Indeed, the ambition is to replace or transform the domination of technocracy and bureaucracy over the area of
moral-practical life into a relationship of constructive me-
diation. Wellmer (1985:63) suggests that this notion
should be made concrete in an institutional setting:

> The formalized processes of administration,
> legislation, and jurisdiction would... enter into
> a new constellation with nonformalized -- or
> not necessarily formalized -- processes of com-
> munication and will-formation, *so that* the
> formalized decision processes would become
> permeable to the need-interpretations, moral
> impulses, or aesthetic experiences articulated
> beneath the level of formal organizations.

[12] In the case of government, systematic discourse should
be organized across agencies and their networks of interests and expertise, for example, between agencies
responsible for industry and economic growth and
those responsible for environment and the quality of
life. The competitive process would serve to stimulate
and sustain administrative dynamism (as markets do
to some extent in the case of private enterprises.

[13] Majone (1986:37-38) observes:

> Finally, it is important to note that in a de-
> mocracy persuasion is (or at least can be) a
> process of mutual education. Keynes's con-
> tributions to the public debate on the prob-
> lems of wartime finance in the late 1930s
> are an excellent example of this process. In
> addition to producing a stream of memo-

randa, articles, broadcasts and letters to the press, Keynes held numerous meetings with officials, politicians, students and trade union leaders. As a result of these discussions, he introduced several modifications into his original scheme for deferred pay on compulsory savings, such as family allowances to protect the low paid with large families, stabilization of the prices of the basic items of consumption, and a post-war capital levy to repay the compulsory savings and redistribute wealth. Thus modified in a process of debate and persuasion, his proposals gained wide acceptance. The 1941 Budget (of the U.K.) , which set the pattern for all subsequent wartime financial policy, was truly Keynesian in inspiration and presentation.

5

SYSTEMATIC DEMOCRATIC DISCOURSE: ISSUES, LEGITIMACY, AND POWER

In this chapter we examine several of the characteristic features of systematic democratic discourse in the context of contemporary politics.

5.1   APPROPRIATE ISSUES FOR SYSTEMATIC DEMOCRATIC DISCOURSE

Systematic democratic discourse -- is designed for -- is particularly appropriate for settings where politics and science meet or should meet, namely, where legal and policy decisions about new technological developments, the establishment and elaboration of new sociotechnical systems, or other policy decisions entailing considerable technical and scientific knowledge are made, or should be made.

Such settings combine "genuine political context" and "technical context." Nurmi (1984:329) points out:

> (I)n genuinely political contexts, the victory of one's own candidate or favourite policy is important *per se,* while the way in which it is achieved -- as long as strict legality is observed -- is of secondary importance. In expert groups, on the other hand, one could more easily entertain the

128

assumption that the group members are committed to finding the "right" alternative. To the extent that they think a procedure leads to the right alternative, there is a presumption that they reveal their preferences and weight assignments sincerely. In politics, in contrast, there is typically no commonly shared assumption that there exists a right alternative. It follows then that there can be no commitment to a procedure by virtue of its alleged result in a *right* outcome.

The issues for systematic discourse are those relating to proposals -- or questions of continuation -- of sociotechnical systems that have, or threaten to have, major impacts on the social and natural environments. Such systems also entail the substantial use of resources, capital investments, expertise, and political legitimation.

Major decisions and public policy made completely in political terms without regard to expert knowledge (no matter how shaky and tentative) are likely to lead to ineffective and, in some instances, even disastrous policies and dangerous sociotechnical systems. The history of government policy shows many examples of policies and programs that were believed to be effective and enjoyed a high level of consensus when, in fact, the belief was not at all justified.

TABLE 4.1 Incentive Conditions, Conflict Intensity, and Feasibility of Successful Democratic Discourse

CONFLICT CONDITIONS

Incentive Conditions	Issues Or Areas With Low Value Or Normative Conflict	Intense Conflicts Over Values And/Or Strategies
	TYPE I	TYPE II
LOW COOPERATIVE INCENTIVES OR PAYOFFS[1]	Discussion may take place but no sustained discourse oriented to decision and action	Discourse and negotiation difficult to sustain, very unstable. This is the case of value conflict with no external threat or opportunity for major mutual gains. Ex: Protestant/Catholic in Northern Ireland, some of the contending parties in Lebanon.
	TYPE III	TYPE IV
HIGH COOPERATIVE INCENTIVES OR PAYOFFS	Maximum opportunity for systematic democratic discourse	Possibilities for systematic democratic discourse, but unstable. Tension between payoff structure encouraging engagement and value conflict evoking tension and separation. Flip-flop behavior, piecemeal processes.

[1]This may mean either that the area is not one of substantial payoffs or that outcomes can be determined by the agents individually, without cooperation.

Systematic democratic discourse, as proposed in Chapter 4, would be most appropriate and practical whenever one or more of the following conditions obtains:

1. The issues or actions are largely conducted according to "consensus politics," such as national security policy in many countries;

2. An entirely new set of issues arises, such as those concerning genetic engineering, for which fixed positions among established political groups and parties have not been articulated or developed;

3. The issues or actions are ones about which political parties and major political groups have no agreed-on positions because of internal disagreements concerning the issues;

4. The issues and perspectives on the issues are shifting and political parties and major groups are interested in exploring new positions and perspectives.

5. The issues are controversial within scientific communities, where groups of scientists seek backing by a broader public or political agents, as in the case today of genetic engineering in West Germany.

Even in cases where opposing positions are well established, there may be substantial incentives for negotiating and reaching agreement that provide advantageous circumstances for organizing democratic discourse (see Table 5.1)[1]. Such cases are most likely to arise in action settings in which the actions of different agents are interdependent and uncoordinated independent choices lead to outcomes that are worse for all. More optimal outcomes can be achieved through coordination and collective decision making. Included here are cases of the unintended depletion of a scarce common or collective good such as water, forests, or some other natural resource that occurs because individuals are free to pursue self-interested resource exploitation and to generate pollution (that is, the "commons problem" (Hardin 1972; Burns et al, 1985)).

Collective agreements may be also motivated by a shared desire to mobilize sufficient sufficient to produce particular collective goods -- an energy system, a transport system, or a military defense force -- that could not be produced or purchased otherwise. Through collective agreements, a community or group establishes norms or legitimate rules prescribing contributions and proscribing free-riding and cheating. In the absence of such enforced norms and organizing principles, people would fail to realize opportunities for gain or risk collective failure as a result of the inability to work together or to sustain cooperation.

Organized democratic discourse is most appropriate in situations where the issues, while possibly evoking a majority-minority split, do not readily resolve themselves in majority/minority domination. Such situations may arise because the minorities are essential to legitimation of the decision, mobilization of resources, or practical implementation. In many cases, intense value conflicts underlie the positions of different actors or groups with regard to such topics as nuclear energy, disposal of nuclear waste, fast-breeder reactors, deployment of the Pershing II missile, Star Wars (Strategic Defense Initiative, or SDI). Specific issues usually reflect only the tip of an iceberg with much more profound issues and deep value conflicts. This is certainly the case with arguments for or against nuclear energy or for or against new weapon systems such as SDI entails. The actors involved, however, may not realize, at least very clearly, what new systemic alternatives are being proposed, or what differences there are between one alternative and another.

In such cases, *democratic decision making according to majority rule does not resolve the basic issues or underlying conflicts.* A simple majority-minority relationship and domination may be precarious, or over the long run highly unstable, and prone to escalating conflict. In cases where an intense minority is determined to block or undermine a majority policy or project, it simply may not be possible to effectively or reasonably implement it over the long run. The demand for higher degrees of consensus and legitimation calls for negotiation and exploration of acceptable systemic alternatives.

In instances where elementary forms of democratic discourse have already been initiated, the question of appropriateness and cost may never arise. In any case, our model suggests ways to effectively organize the process and increase its efficiency.

However, attempts to initiate democratic discourse in settings where there is little or no tradition of democratic discourse, where a single or majority line uniquivocally dominates, or where technocratic decision making prevails, are likely to meet serious resistance. Vested interests as well as those concerned with matters of efficiency will stress the costs, likelihood of delays, and disruption resulting from "further talk."

Certainly, democratic discourse concerning alternative sociotechnical futures entails substantial costs. First, it costs the time and energy of those directly responsible for decision making, who participate in a more open, less predictable process. It also entails the cost of the additional expertise that usually must be mobilized to articulate and develop previously neglected alternative concepts or systems. Such costs are likely to be even greater during a period of initial learning and development of the techniques of democratic discourse in areas of technology and science. Presently, we lack sustained, cumulative experience and established institutional forms. Policymakers and experts must still acquire the spectrum of skills and process knowledge essential to effective democratic discourse.

Quite clearly, *one would not initiate such a process except in areas where the stakes are high, for instance, if the resource investments are very large. Or if the impacts of the actions taken on the* social and natural environments may *be substantial and may possibly have irreversible consequences.* We have in mind large-scale energy systems, hazardous waste disposal, large-scale computerization of factories and offices, telecommunication systems, genetic engineering development, and radically new, potentially destabilizing national defense systems.

The costs of organizing and sustaining systematic democratic discourse in the case of major or radical sociotechnical developments would be only a *small fraction of the actual project investments* (a few million dollars as compared to the hundreds of millions and even billions of dollars for many modern sociotechnical developments). The costs for financing and organizing systematic democratic discourse are relatively marginal compared to the monetary and non-monetary risks involved in such undertakings. In our view, most citizens would be prepared to bear these marginal costs in taxation, just as they are largely willing to pay the salaries of elected officials and the other costs of a functioning democracy.

Already today in the United States, the National Environmental Policy Act (NEPA) requires that any proposal for a federal project or program consider also the altenative of "no project" or "continuation of current practice." In particular, federal agencies are required to "(A) utilize a systematic, interdisciplinary approach which will insure the integrated use of the natural and social sciences and the environmental design arts in planning and decision making which may have an impact on man's environment" and "(B) identify methods and procedures... which will insure that presently unquantified environmental amenities and values may be given appropriate consideration in decision making along with economic and technical consideration." (as quoted in Dietz,1987:57-58). Such legal requirements, and the concrete application of impact assessment, could be readily extended to cover consideration of systemic alternatives, thus going beyond the restriction limiting consideration to only the no-project or current-practice alternatives.

Democratic discourse, as we have conceptualized it, does not make sense if decisions must be made very quickly, or a moratorium on making a decision can scarcely be tolerated for the length of time required to carry out the entire process, or previous decisions and policies are largely irreversible (see Table 5.2)[2].

TABLE 5.2:
TIME PERSPECTIVE, PROBLEM SITUATION AND TYPE OF DECISION

TYPE OF PROBLEM SITUATION

TIME PERSPECTIVE

	SIMPLE, LOW TECH	COMPLEX, HIGH TECH
SHORT-TERM	Routine administrative and/or political decision-making	Crisis Management and decision-making
LONG-TERM	Same as above, with possibly more stress on the political	DEMOCRATIC DISCOURSE

In some instances, well-established sociotechnical systems are considered by societal actors and political interests as, for all practical purposes, *irreversible developments*. We should bear in mind, nonetheless, that even apparently irreversible developments have been politically reversed on occasion. Sweden, for example, had until recently the world's most amibitious nuclear program and a high level of nuclear energy production (with 12 very large reactors in a country with a population of 8 million). In 1980, in connection with a national referendum, the decision was made to devolve nuclear power within 25 years.

To sum up, systematic democratic discourse is suitable for problem situations in which the actors are strongly disposed to engage in negotiation of issues and to try to reach settlements[3]. (a) The participants are faced with a clear choice, either to make a collective decision and to engage in the necessary discourse and consensus building essential to accomplish that or to run the very high economic, environmental, or political risks associated with a failure to make a collective decision, for example, concerning alternative energy systems. (b) The problem is not simply a technical one. Rather, the legitimate or proposed alternative is perceived by at least some groups as leading to what might eventually be highly risky or unacceptable outcomes. (c) The time frame for collective decision making allows for organizing and carrying out a process of systematic discourse and even, in some cases, the reversal of major decisions made earlier.

5.2   DISCOURSE SETTINGS

Democratic discourse in the form outlined in Chapter 4 may be initiated in a variety of political settings and public forums. The following are some examples:

1. In a *legislative,* in which initially a committee consisting of representatives of different perspectives and approaches (caucus, party, or block) assumes or is given responsibility to initiate and carry out investigations and discussions con-

cerning major technological issues or developments[4]. One can find this already being done in many enquiries and policy processes, but the process should be specified and understood more explicitly, and practical knowledge of it developed further and institutionalized.

Consider the case of the Commission on "Future Energy Politics" of the German Parliament (German Parliament, 1980, 2 volumes), which suggests some of the realistic possibilities for systematic democratic discourse. The commission, chaired by one of the authors (Ueberhorst), consisted of members of Parliament (from all parties) and various experts qualified with differing viewpoints concerning the assessment of nuclear energy and its future role in Germany.

The commission decided, and carried through work, on long-term systemic alternatives relating to different energy futures under differing economic and resource conditions. By means of systematic discourse, the commission established a framework for analysis and explored future energy altenatives. Moreover, it eventually reached a set of majority conclusions and recommendations by the vote of 12 to three. This happened although the commission was divided from the beginning on the issue of nuclear energy, with ten of the fifteen members in favor of it. All five of the initial opponents were a part of the final majority of 12.

2. *Government agencies* -- with their networks of external advisers and contacts -- are responsible for certain policy areas and initiate a democratic discourse process. Or, they are asked by the political leadership or legislature to make policy proposals. They would be expected to recruit actors with differing, and even opposing, perspectives on an issue.

3. Representative bodies as well as government agencies may set up special hearings or inquiries in connection with a major project or proposal. There are a number of examples of such public discussion, for instance, the Berger inquiry into the Mackenzie Valley pipeline (Gamble, 1978; Dietz, 1987).

The inquiry provided a forum for sustained public debate on the pipeline. It sponsored well-publicized hearings and *provided funds to organizations interested in participating.* Dietz (1987:61) notes:

> The process was very successful at opening up debate on a large complex project. As Gamble (1978:951) concludes, the inquiry "... demonstrates that the obligation of the expert in industry and government is to expose, at a very early stage, the whole range of issues to the "expert" scrutiny of all citizens. The citizens" input has now been shown to be essential to an assessment process." This general approach to facilitating public scrutiny and debate has also been used successfully in the evaluations of Community Development Block Grants and in the evaluation of proposed urban developments.

In our view, the tradition of public inquiries and public hearings provides an excellent frame for organizing and carrying out systematic discussion on alternative proposals and developments.

4. *Inter-organizational settings* such as tripartite organizations (involving representatives of business, labor and government) are important forums in which to set in motion sustained and systematic discourse about major sociotechnical developments. Labor representatives are likely to have a different idea of the future organization of an industry (or of office or service work) than representatives of management. This would provide a reason for engaging in a discourse in which alternatives concerning future technological developments, work organization, and employment are articulated and systematically developed.

5. *Religious organizations and movement organizations,* which in many instances are motivated to establish political discourse, already play or can play a substantial role in organizing discourses concerning alternative technological futures with respect to nuclear energy, genetic engineering, and human reproduction. The central labor unions in Sweden have started to do this with respect to biotechology developments.

6. *Universities, research institutions and professional groups* initiate a process of systematic democratic discourse, possibly in order to open to public scrutiny and debate issues or conflicts among members of the scientific community, drawing in, for instance, political leaders and representatives of business and labor. Stern (1987: 29) points out the role that institutions such as the Scientists' Institute for Public Information play in helping journalists identify opposing sides and find articulate advocates for each. He adds (1987:29-30):

> (...) it may be useful sometimes to draw on the old idea of a science court, not to reach final decisins on matters of fact as if they can be sharply distinguished from matters of value, but to provide citizens with a new information source...

7. *Mass media organisations* take the initiative in organizing such processes. This would of course go far beyond a series of debates among advocates of the different positions, in that systemic alternatives would be articulated and developed with the assistance of experts. The media would be most likely to do this in the case of major public controversies: conflicts over nuclear energy, transportation systems, health care, genetic engineering, etc.

8. In *local communities* citizens, political groupings, and other interests come together to decide on a course of action concerning, for instance, alternative uses of natural resourc-

es (land, forests, water, etc.), waste disposal proposals, local employment and development schemes (Kemmis, 1987). They organize their discussions and decision making according to the principles of systematic democratic discourse.

Typically, the discourse process works better, at least in some phases, with smaller groups and assemblies. Representatives of larger groups can participate in smaller forums, but with, for instance, full video coverage of the discourse process and with discourses organized as well in networks of related settings and in larger groupings[5]. Modern telecommunications offer excellent opportunities for the development of systematic discourse about major issues.

The above is meant to be suggestive. Certainly, a variety of settings and combinations of participants are conceivable. These will vary considerable by country, region, and community; each has its own political forms and forums, its particular political agents and styles. The main task, in our view, is to get on with the task of organizing and institutionalizing systematic discussion and analysis of sociotechnical futures. This will enable politicians and citizens to better discern issues and problems relating to new technologies, major technological developments, and the risks as well as challenges involved in these.

5.3 LEGITIMACY AND CONSENSUS

A new social form for democratic discourse should enjoy the legitimacy of democracy and, therefore, should be acceptable to all who out of conviction, or social pressure, adhere to democratic principles and values.

Consensus, in a certain sense, is required. But democratic discourse concerns, above all, consensus about *the form of a social process: the organizing principles, procedures, and strategies* for democratic discourse[6].

Democratic discourse does not refer to eventual consensus among the participants about the appropriate collective decision or development. In general, *our model does not presume or require consensus about the content of politics.* It would be be illusionary -- and a possible threat to democratic forms -- to expect social actors to agree on the level of issues. However, as stressed earlier, the issues may be ones for which a high degree of consensus is required in order to deal effectively with the relevant problems. The possibility of some degree of consensus formation becomes a reality, or in some instances at least likely, in part due to the organization of the discourse process and systematic discussion.

Our proposal is not idealism dressed up in the robes of science. Human institutions are nether more nor less than organizing principles and rules -- particular social forms -- about which some degree of consensus must obtain among the participants. But any social form that is to be institutionalized in the modern world should, on the one hand, enjoy wide support or legitimacy. On the other hand, it should be realistic in its consideration of established patterns of everyday life: institutionalized conflicts, organized interests, and political parties.

Systematic democratic discourse would become a creative social force to the extent that actors involved or affected feel obliged or motivated to adhere to the organizing principles and rules[7]. A variety of factors may operate here. (a) The organizing principles and rules prevail, either legally or as part of an established political culture. (b) Public opinion, pressure groups and mediating actors enforce a certain minimum level of adherence; (c) Processes of argument, persuasion, arm-twisting, etc., that are part and parcel of politics are well-developed means to assure a minimum level of success essential to the vitality of any institution. And (d) certain types of power -- violence, bureaucratic power, and control of property -- are to a greater or lesser extent excluded from the discourse, as stressed earlier.

5.4   EQUALITY AND INSTITUTIONAL POWER DIFFERENCES

Strictly speaking, democratic discourse and negotiation, as general social forms, are incompatible with, and cannot be applied in, bureaucratic and purely technocratic settings[8]. The process is organized so that the participation of technical expertise does not lead to technocratic dominance, whereby technical elites set aside or compromise democratic discourse and decision making.

Although the actors are in formal terms equal with respect to organizing principles and rules of democratic discourse, inequality among the actors is a persistent problem. It cannot be eliminated except at the expense of other institutions that are socially important and that, in paradoxical ways, may contribute to strengthening democracy. For instance, family, private property, and local community countervail to some extent the domination of the state; the state itself may defend individuals against the domination of private property interests or powerful local communities and groups.

The actors bring into ostensibly democratic discussions decision-making power resources, including property, institutional roles, and network positions that to a greater or lesser extent serve as factors of power that compromise or limit democratically organized processes. The actors vary not only in the degree of their visible resource control, owing to institutional differences in the authority and power of their positions, but also in their levels of knowledge, skills, and expertise. Thus, they will vary in their ability to identify and construct systemic alternatives. They will also vary in their skills in questioning and evaluating the soundness or legitimacy of other proposed alternatives and in their capacity to engage in discourse processes and to mobilize support for a proposal or argument.

In a world of high science and technology, technical expertise is essential to democratic discussion and decision making. Certainly, democracy, like any other type of political decision-making process, is largely uninformed or misinformed concerning questions of technology and science. Unless this problem can be overcome, the result will be unsound laws, policies, and programs -- in some instances with potentially disastrous consequences. In many instances, *technocracy contradicts democratic discourse as we envision it, since* technocracy works hand and glove with *those wishing to select and implement a single systemic alternative.* Moreover, engineers and scientists often ignore the social and political limitations of deciding and implementing a systemic alternative without genuine democratic discourse and negotiation. Substantial political and economic costs may have to be paid after the project is well under way.

Democratic discourse can and should utilize expert knowledge -- in particular in the formulation and analysis of systemic alternatives, and in designing and carrying out concrete discourse procedures. Through defining more clearly the relationship between experts and democratic agents and organizing democratic discourse around multiple options, technocracy can be more effectively subordinated to democracy without at the same time jeopardizing the integrity and discipline of expert knowledge.

5.5   PRACTICAL, NOT PURE REASON

The model of systematic democratic discourse does not assume that either the actors are rational or the process is rational in some ideal sense. The form is a means of organizing and carrying out discourse and negotiation among agents who are equal at least in constitutional terms. Discourse as a social form is designed to be as reasonable and effective as possible. We do not presume or expect that the participants will always reach a consensus[9].

Democratic discourse is more then than "discussion;" it is oriented to collective decision making and collective action. In this sense, it is more instrumental than discussion as such. It is also different from rules of debate. Political debate entails presentation and defense of positions (as in legislatures in plenary session, United Nations sessions, etc.). The rules of the political game -- the very nature of the social form -- do not allow argumentation to lead to any fundamental change in the positions of the parties or to the systematic formulation or discovery of new alternatives. At any rate, these results are not promoted in an institutionalized manner. A decisionmaker or policymaker finds it appropriate, under these conditions, to stick to a defined position. Such a stance also avoids problems among those represented or internal to the organization or group represented. This conservatism is part and parcel of run-of-the-mill or routine politics.

Democratic discourse consists, in part, of collective problem-solving processes. Its realization is intended not only to satisfy certain fundamental normative principles relating to the relationships among human beings but also to contribute to establishing or extending a collective capability or power. In this sense, it is *practical and instrumental.* It enables a group, organization, or other collectivity to address or solve certain problems, to mobilize resources to purchase or to produce a good, or to establish norms and coordination procedures for resolving collective action problems and social conflicts. A more or less heterogenous group -- that is, made up of persons or subgroups with different ideas, conceptions, values, and strategic orientation -- may be able to engage, interact, and produce solutions to problems by virtue of the organizational strategy and the particular methods associated with systematic democratic discourse.

In short, we believe that by instituting new forms of democratic activity, we believe that it is possible to deal more effectively with the complex, often technically complex, issues and questions that confront human societies today.

5.6 CONVENTIONAL PARTY POLITICS AND DEMOCRATIC DISCOURSE

The organizing principles and rules of the game governing political parties in modern democracies contradict in a certain sense the principles of democratic discourse. Many if not most Western political parties are hierarchical in character, the notable exception being the Democratic and Republican parties of the United States (which have their own special problems in a political arena often characterized as profoundly "Hollywoodish" in character). Some European parties, for example, the Christian Democrats of Germany, have never had an internal discussion on nuclear power or a conceptualization of systemic alternatives concerning the use of nuclear energy. In general, the higher up in a party one goes, the more homogeneous the manner of viewing societal problems. Interactions between parties tend to be competitive and oppositional, not compositional (Ueberhorst, 1985b). Genuine political discourse and creativity are often retarded or altogether blocked.

In a democracy, politicians and their parties acquire the power to make decisions by successfully competing for people's votes. They are not rewarded particularly for clarifying issues, but for mobilizing votes. Since they want to appeal to as many people as possible, they will, whenever feasible, avoid expressing a clear position that might alienate those who have other positions but would otherwise vote for them. Typically, they will try to stick to the sorts of statements that will maximize votes, for instance, statements about high-valence issues (peace, prosperity, goodwill, national dignity, and honor), or which will solidify support in certain constituencies. Presentations of clearly formulated alternatives, or the formulation of genuinely new alternatives, are, in many instances, not the best strategies to use in order to maximize or consolidate votes. Consequently, the establishment and development of new forms of democratic discourse are not likely to be greatly facilitated or reinforced by traditional party politics and conventional rules of the political game.

Political parties are, of course, relevant and important agents in modern democracies and must be taken into account in any design of democratic discourse. Presently, they develop their own concepts, language, and programs, in part in order to maintain or articulate their distinct identities. Indeed, certain concepts, a special language, and a set of programs constitute, in large part, their identity. Identities, commitments, internal discipline, and established positions on issues are activated, above all, in public settings, including elections.

Conventional modern politics is strongly competitive as a consequence of the rules of the game and the social formations within which politics is played out. These practices have a well-established role in Western politics and policy making as we know it. Our proposal is intended to complement, not to eliminate, these more conventional games. In this sense, it is a modest proposal, although the ambition is radical.

The widespread diffusion of forms of democratic discourse might serve to enhance or reinforce the internal democratization of political parties, particularly with regard to local and "small-community issues" on which the majority of the parties' members have not developed clear-cut positions. Even in inter-party arenas, the model could contribute to a shift in the political rules of the game away from rigid competitive politics toward more flexible forms of collective decision making and action, particularly in policy areas concerned with technology, science, and national security.

5.7 VALUES AND DEMOCRATIC MORALITY

Questions of values and morality are central to democratic discourse. Basic values enter into the design of sociotechnical alternatives. They also tend to be exposed through the expression of concerns about impacts of particular sociotechnical systems, and through systematic discourse and negotiation. In general, democratic discourse can provide a public setting for articulating, discussing, and learning about fundamental values in a society.

The very organization of democratic discourse, as outlined in Chapter 4, embody key moral principles and values. That is, there must be -- or must be established -- a meta-morality underlying specific group, class, or community moralities. In part, this is the principle of mutual respect and equality and the shared aim of trying to understand and to reach agreements with one another. Breach of such norms undermines or aborts democracy as a general form for social life.

5.8   CONCLUSION

In concluding, we want to stress the concrete, practical aspects of our proposal to increase democratic discourse and control relating to major sociotechnical developments.

First, we have suggested a particular social form or paradigm: systematic democratic discourse. The proposal is more than simply a call for greater discussion or more debate about issues relating to scientific and technological developments, although such public activity would certainly be worthwhile. Our proposal concerns: (1) systematically organizing the formulation of alternative sociotechnical systems and (2) organizing sustained public consideration of alternative sociotechnical futures. This form of public activity should, in our view, be fully institutionalized in democratic societies, in part through legal and budgetary authorizations, as outlined below.

The model of democratic discourse proposed is intended to contribute specifically to:

- A greater democratization of technological innovation and development, particularly in large-scale systems[10]

- A systematic linking of the spectrum of human values to technical, scientific, and, in general, factual knowledge;

- The creative generation of alternatives

- Mutual understanding and consensus formation;

- Negotiation and collective decision making.

Organized democratic discourse stresses the generation of alternatives: in part to demonstrate concretely and practically that there are always alternative technological possibilities and alternative technological futures; in part to avoid pitfalls that cause actors to become unnecessarily locked into their positions or to ignore scientific or technical knowledge that has a bearing on the formulation and impact assessment of systemic alternatives; in part to expose underlying values and assumptions and to faciliate social learning and consensus formation on deeper levels of human value structures.

While competing alternatives are characteristic of the model, it differs from purely competitive politics, where the point is to win votes. It also differs from a purely adversary relation in that participants are challenged to reach agreement on major future developments. Of course, disagreements and social conflict are inherent features of such processes, but there are powerful incentives to explore and develop alternatives that command wide support, even consensus.

Finally, the organizational form concretizes the process of *integrating* public values and scientific and technical knowledge (the "pragmatic mode" in Habermas' terms as discussed on page 69). It defines the limited, but essential, role of experts in relation to those with political authority to decide. Persons representing different values and commitments are to be involved in these undertakings. It is not enough that technicians and other experts try to act as representatives on behalf of imagined or imaginary "publics."

Second, we have stressed the importance of utilizing and developing public forums of discussion *outside the usual party political forums:* among others, special hearings and inquiries, inter-organizational settings such as tripartite bodies, labor union associations, university and professional group settings, and communities (particularly in instances where the communities are likely to be affected by major technological deveopments).

The development of such forums would serve not only to increase the number and variety of settings in which sustained and systematic public consideration of technological futures takes place but also to effect a qualitative shift in the major locus of public discussion from competitive party settings to those in which manifold social vaues and alternative conceptions may be brought into sustained and creative dialogue with one another. This serves to break the discourse out of the confines of narrow political arenas where the rules of the political game mitigate against sustained, systematic consideration of, and dialogue about, alternative sociotechnical futures.

We have not claimed that the model of democratic discourse should or can replace the spectrum of forms in which contemporary politics is carried out. As a complement to these, the model may be established and institutionalized in various public settings outside of, for instance, election arenas and official parliamentary debates and votes where conventional party politics typically prevail.

Third, we propose that public funds be allocated for the purpose of carrying out organized discourse about alternative sociotechnical futures. This should include funding to make possible the systematic formulation of alternative proposals. This is especially important *whenever the matters concern large-scale projects or projects and developments with potential major impact on the physical and social environment.*

The funding would enable the mobilization of necessary technical, economic, legal, and other kinds of expertise to systematically investigate and formulate alternative proposals. This is essential when one sociotechnical development or proposed system already has the backing of major economic and government interests and no sensible or viable alternative appears available. We firmly believe that such a proposal in the name of democracy -- and the modernization and revitalizationa of democracy -- would find wide support.

Fourth, we propose that income to finance the formulation of sociotechnical alternatives and sustained public discussion be based on an *automatic mechanism* rather than annual public budget allocations. The latter are subject to political whims as well as systematic manipulation.

We suggest that a public fund or foundation be established, to be financed out of general tax revenues or a special tax -- for instance a 1-2 percent tax -- on all research and development (R&D) investments, including those of the military. These resources would be made available to alternative formulations and discourse processes, for instance those organized in the types of settings referred to earlier. In some cases, such as large-scale projects and developments, alternative formulations and discourse should be legally required in a manner similar to the present requirement in the United States that the proposal of any federal project or program take into consideration at the same time the alternative of "no project" or "continuation of current practice," as specified by the National Environmental Policy Act. In other cases, groups of policymakers and citizens who are concerned about certain technical developments such as genetic engineering could apply for grants to initiate discourse activities; these would be organized in accordance with principles outlined in Chapter 4.

Democratic discourse is already practiced today in a variety of decision-making contexts in most if not all modern Western societies. What is lacking, however, is a full awareness of what some of the practices entail, what their full potentialities are, and how they can be further institutionalized and developed as major social forms. Such development is a challenge to us all -- it may also enable us to find paths to survival in a world of high science and technology.

NOTES

[1] As Table 5.1 suggests, some cases of opposition (Type II)
     provide few incentives for activating and carrying
     through democratic discourse. Systematic structuring of
     incentives and payoffs would offer some hope (for in-
     stance, moving the actors from Type II to Type IV).
     We want to stress the importance of specifying
     the conditions for more or less effective democratic dis-
     course and the types of vulnerabilities and buffering
     and countering strategies that should be recognized if
     the process is to be sustained. Concerning Habermas's
     more idealistic conception, we find ourselves agreeing to
     a certain extent with Andersson and Davis (1981:214):

> Generally speaking, when codes for speak-
> ing and interpretation are tied to absolutist
> polarities like good and evil, right and
> wrong, holiness and sin, we should expect
> the cognitive activities of code-brokers to be
> of limited usefulness. Habermas's utopia of
> social problem solving through the con-
> struction of situations in which the social
> and semantic barriers to communication --
> status differences, differences in linguistic
> competence -- have been removed may be
> realizable only in those cases where these
> polarities are not activated.

Nevertheless, the history of war and diplomacy points up
that even in the case of highly polarized groups or nations,
some degree of dialogue and negotiation is achievable. Of
course, this is most likely in instances in which there are

152

powerful incentives to avoid substantial losses or to make great gains. This indicates the urgency of examining empirical cases and developing theories relating to Type IV.

[2] This argument concerns the general principle that any social procedure is likely to be evaluated according to several criteria. In that case, democratic principles or values are not the only basis of assessment. Criteria of cost and efficiency also come into consideration, as suggested above.

[3] Relevant here also are international negotiations between sovereign states, where no "solution" or action can be found if one of the main participants opposes or abstains. The following situations are important instances:

[4] The report of the German Parliament's Commission of Inquiry, *Technology Assessment and Evaluation: Creating the Basic Conditions for Technical Progress,* stresses the potential role of the legislature in such processes:

> A large number of political concepts and programmes still seem to be dominated by the standpoint that the chosen path for modernizing the economy and society by more technology is a relatively explicit line of approach characterized by certain technical constraints. *The consciousness of the options and differing approaches available in the processes inherent in the genesis, introduction and use of technologies has not yet been sufficiently developed or translated into political action. None the less, there are in fact wider areas for action and organization and more varied lines of development than people often assume or claim to exist.*

One of Parliament's overall tasks lies in making this discernible and familiar in addition to discussing the instruments to be employed. This must take place irrespective of the fact that the Parliament consists of members from competing parties with different political concepts. (German Parliament, 1986:39)

[5] As Frohlich and Oppenheimer (1978:97) point out in discussing the different qualities of the decision-making process in small groups and organizations and larger colleciivities:

Committees adopt rules and legislation with many possible options and details, all decided upon by complicated series of votes. An electorate usually has a more restricted function: to decide between vaguely and ambiguously defined alternatives. An electorate rarely has more to say about these alternatives than "yea" or "nay."

[6] As Wellmer (1985:59) points out about Habermas concerning a certain level of consensus on basic norms, institutions, and values:

Certainly nothing prevents us from assuming that part of this consensus is a principle saying that in cases of disagreement on practical matters, agreement ought to be brought about by argument as much as possible. Under these conditions, communicative action *might* become the primary mechanism of action coordination. This does not necessarily mean that there are, e.g. no majority decisions; it simply means that in cases of normative disagreement some kind of agreement is brought about which is considered as "fair" or "just" by all individuals involved (e.g., that a majority vote should be taken and accepted by all). This means, evidently, that nobody is *forced* to do or to tolerate what he is not convinced he/she should (morally should) do or tolerate. By free agreements we mean, of course, agreements which are not the result of manipulation or internalized pressure.

[7] In contrast to Habermas, we do not seek the basis of consensus in the very structure of communication, but we see consensus as both normatively and instrumentally based. Consensus is not a given; its existence is precarious and calls for struggle and "eternal vigilance."

We cannot consider here in any systematic way the proposition of Habermas that the very structure of language expresses unequivocally the intention of universal and unrestricted consensus, a consensus realizable only in an emancipated society.

This is a questionable proposition, in part because of the obvious fact that human communication is used for and in domination and repression. Some actors are in a better position to impose their "logic" on others, thus excluding or minimizing "dialogical forms."

The key to "conditioning" rational discussion in a Habermasian sense are *the social norms of reciprocity and equality that constitute particular social relations, that is, a social structure,* rather than a language structure (See Burns and Flam 1987 for models of the structure of communication in domination relations.)

At the same time, there are social forms for communication among equals, as formulated in "systematic
democratic discourse," where "consensus formation"
presupposes in many instances discussions among free
and equal persons and, therefore, an emancipated society free from repression and domination. That is, social
structure antedates communication structures, at the
same time that the latter contribute to the reproduction
of the former.

In our view, Habermas fails to specify real institutional
and organizational potentialities in the modern world --
a concrete historical situation -- to overcome technocratic and bureaucratic domination, among other things
(Bernstein, 1985a:7).

Wellmer (1985: 59) critically examines utopian ration-
alism, an "idealized life world," in the following terms:

> (D)emocratic legitimacy, although it must
> be conceived of as being based on a consen-
> sus of basic norms, institutions, and values,
> cannot be understood as being based on a
> *rational* consensus. The upshot of this criti-
> cism is that communicative action and ra-
> tional discourse ultimately cannot generate
> legitimate institutions (legitimate power),
> but that only legitimate institutions (legiti-
> mate power) could set free communicative
> action as a mechanism of social coordina-
> tion. As far as the legitimacy of institutions
> is concerned, however, there can be no ideal
> limit; there is rather an irreducible element
> of "voluntas" as against "ratio," or, to put
> it in Hannah Arendt's terms, legitimate
> power can only be based on "opinion." This
> means, however, that (1) there is no inter-
> nal link between the ideas of rationality and

radical democracy, and (2) that normative idealizations like that of an "idealized life-world" are, strictly speaking, meaningless. In sort, there is no *rational* solution to the problem of an institutionalization of freedom.

[8] Moreover, democratic discourse and negotiation should be applicable to negotiative-contractual settings, for example, labor-management negotiations, as well as international forums to the extent that the actors involved participate as equals and adhere to democratic principles of discourse and negotiation. To the extent that negotiation and contractual agreements exclude important actors -- third parties -- affected by the process, they violate a fundamental principle of democracy, the right of those affected by a collective decision or action to participate in and to influence the decision making and action.

[9] The agreement is not anchored in the various opinions of participants but in the very form organizing and regulating their ongoing activities (Burns and Flam, 1987). We presume that diversity of opinion is endemic to social life. There is not, and cannot be, a universal intersubjective consensus, that is, an eventual agreement among all opinions on a rational basis (cf. Habermas, 1984; Apel, 1979)).

One of our basic premises is that human actors come to better understand themselves and one another through engagement in dialogue. Exposure to conflicting values and purposes and different strategies contributes to social learning and the capability to generate new alternatives. Social institutions such as those designed to enable negotiation of conflicts and engagement in discussion, argument, and the presentation of evidence make consensus formation more likely or effective.

We recognize that a more cynical approach, with a stress on high ambiguity and deception, may also contribute to dampening or limiting conflict potential -- at least in the short run.

[10] The proposal can be seen as entailing a synthesis of competing forms and orientations, a synthesis that retains the integrity of the forms: purposive-instrumental rationality and moral-value rationality. Put in another way, one might, following Habermas, consider the interplay between the world of "systematic instrumental rationality" and the "life-world" (Lebenswelt) of the human taken-for-granted universe of daily social activity (traditions, established ways of doing things, diffuse values and norms; morality as opposed to legality). Wellmer (1985:58) refers to the "problem of an adequate objectification of communicative rationality in new and political institutions, i.e., ones which on the one hand, would represent the normative anchoring of the system in the life-world, and, on the other, would protect the communicative structures of the life-world themselves and secure a rational and democratic control of the system by the life-world.

REFERENCES

Andersson, B. and A. Davis 1981 In Willer and Andersson.

Apel, K-O. 1979 "Types of Social Science in the Light of Human Cognitive Interests." In Brown (ed).

Baumgartner, T. and T.R. Burns 1984 *Transitions to Alternative Energy Systems: Entrepreneurs, New Technologies, and Social Change.* Boulder, Colo., and London: Westview.

Baumgartner, T. *et al* 1986 *The Shaping of Socioeconomic Systems.* London and New York: Gordon and Breach.

Baumgartner, T. and A. Midttun, eds. 1987 *The Politics of Forecasting.* Oxford: Oxford University Press.

Bereano, P. L. 1976 *Technology as a Social and Political Phenomenon.* New York: Wiley.

Bernstein, R.J. 1985a "Introduction." In Bernstein (1985b). 1-34.

Bernstein, R. J., ed. 1985b *Habermas and Modernity.* Oxford: Polity.

Boulding, K. 1964 *The Meaning of the Twentieth Century.* New York: Harper and Row.

Brown, S., ed. 1979 *Philosophical Disputes in the Social Sciences.* Atlantic Highlands, N.J. : Humanities.

Buckley, W. 1973 "Modern Science and Moral Values -- A Systems View." Paper presented at the 2nd International Conference on the Unity of Science, Tokyo, November, 1973.

Bulmer, M 1987. "The Social Sciences and Societal Development: The 1920s and 1930s." Paper presented at international workshop, Social Science and Societal Development, Berlin, January 29-Feburary 1.

Bunge, M. 1981 *Scientific Materialism*. Dordrecht, Netherlands: Reidel.

Burns, T. R. 1985 *Technological Development with Reference to Hydro-power, Nuclear and Alternative Energy Technologies*. Berlin: Wissenschaftszentrum.

Burns, T. R. and H. Flam 1987 *The Shaping of Social Organization: Social Rule System Theory with Applications*. London: Sage.

Burns, T. R. *et al* 1985 *Man, Decisions, Society*. London and New York: Gordon and Breach.

Camilleri, J.A. 1976 *Civilization in Crisis*. Cambridge: Cambridge University Press.

Clark, W. C. and G. Majone 1984 "The Critical Appraisal of Scientific Inquiries with Policy Implications." Laxenburg, Austria: IIASA (International Institute of Applied Systems Analysis) Report.

Coleman, J. S. 1982 *The Asymmetric Society*. Syracuse, N.Y.:Syracuse University Press.

Coppock, R. 1984 *Social Constraints on Technological Progress*. London: Gower Press.

Dahl, R.A. 1982 *Dilemmas of Pluralist Democracy: Autonomy and Control.* New Haven, Conn.: Yale University Press.

-------------- 1976 *Modern Political Analysis.* Englewood Cliffs, N.J.: Prentice-Hall.

Deutsch, K. 1980 "Technology and Social Change: Fundamental Changes in Knowledge, Technology and Society." *Human Systems Management* 1:127-143.

Dietz, T. 1987 "Theory and Method in Social Impact Assessment." *Sociological Inquiry* 57:54-67.

Douglas, M. and A. Wildavsky 1982 *Risk and Culture: An Essay on the Selection of Technical and Environmental Dangers.* Berkeley: University of California Press.

Draper, R. 1985 "The Golden Arm." *New York Review of Books,* October 24, pp. 46-52.

Durbin, P. T., ed. 1978 *Research in Philosophy and Technology.* Vol 1. Greenwich, Conn.: JAI Press.

Ewerlöf, G. 1985 "Artificial Insemination: Legislation and Debate." *Current Sweden,* no. 329 (1985).

Elster, J. 1986 "The Market and the Forum: Three Varieties of Political Theory." In *Foundations of Social Choice Theory,* ed. J. Elster and A. Hylland. Cambridge: Cambridge University Press.

Etzioni, A. 1985 "Barriers between Sociology and Policymaking." *Footnotes,* December Issue, 11.

----------- 1968 *The Active Society: A Theory of Societal and Political Processes.* New York: Free Press.

Frohlich, N. and J.A. Oppenheimer 1978 *Modern Political Economy.* Englewood Cliffs, N.J.: Prentice-Hall.

Gamble, D. 1978 "The Berger Inquiry: An Impact Assessment Process." *Science* 199:946-952.

German Parliament (Deutscher Bundestag) 1986 *Technology Assessment and Evaluation: Creating Conditions for Technical Progress.* Bonn.

van Gunsteren, H. and G. Lock 1977 *Politieke Theorieen.* Alphen aan den Rijn, Netherlands: Samson.

Gustafsson, Bo 1976 "Inside or Outside the Ivory Tower?" In *Uppsala University: 500 years,* Faculty of Social Sciences, Stockholm: Almqvist and Wiksell International.

Habermas, J. 1984 *Theory of Communicative Action.* Oxford: Polity.

---------- 1971 *Knowledge and Human Interests.* Boston: Beacon.

---------- 1970 *Toward a Rational Society.* Boston: Beacon.

Häfele, W. 1963 "Neuartige Wege naturwissenschaftlich-technischer Entwicklung. In *Die Projektwissenschaften: Forschung und Bildung, 17-38.* Munchen: Schriftenreihe des Bundesministers fur wissenschaftliche Forschung.

---------- 1974 "Hypotheticality and the New Challenges: The Pathfinder Role of Nuclear Energy." *Minerva* 10:303-322.

Hardin, G. 1972 *Exploring New Ethics for Survival.* New York: Viking.

Harris, R. L. 1986 "The Impact of the Micro-electronics Revolution on the Basic Structure of Modern Organizations." *Science, Technology, and Human Values* 11: 31-44.

Henshel, R. L. 1978 "Self-Altering Predictions." *Handbook of Futures Research,* ed. J. Fowles. Westport, Conn.: Greenwood Press.

Howard, R. 1982 *Three Faces of Hermaneutics: An Introduction to Current Theories of Understanding.* Berkeley: University of California Press.

Hummon, N. P. 1984 "Organizational Aspects of Technological Change." In Laudan.

Hunt, H. A. and T. Hunt 1983 *Human Resource Implications of Robotics.* Kalamazoo, Mi: Upjohn Institute for Employment Research.

Ignatieff, M. 1984 *The Needs of Strangers.* London: Hogarth.

Jay, M. 1985 "Habermas and Modermism." In Bernstein (1985b), 125-139.

Karpik, L. 1981 "Organizations, Institutions, and History." *Complex Organizations: Critical Perspectives,* ed. M. Zey-Ferrell and M. Aiken. Glenview, Ill.: Scott, Foresman.

Kemmis, D. 1987 *Building on Common Ground: A Community Workbook.* Telluride, Colo.: Telluride Institute.

Kickert, W. 1979 *Organization of Decision-Making: A Systems Theoretical Approach.* Amsterdam: North Holland.

Kollek, R. 1986 "Sicherheitsaspekte der experimentellen Arbeit mit Retroviren." In Kollek, Tappeser, and Altner.

Kollek, R., B. Tappese, and G. Altner eds. 1986 *Die ungeklärten Gefahrenpotentiale der Gentechnologie.* Munich: Schweitzer Verlag.

Krimsky, S. 1982 *Genetic Alchemy. The Social History of Recombinant DNA Controversy.* Cambridge: MIT Press.

Laudan, R., ed. 1984 *The Nature of Technological Knowledge.* Dordrecht, Netherlands: Reidel.

Layton, E. T. 1974 "Technology as Knowledge." *Technology and Culture* 15:31-42.

Leontief, W. and F. Duchin 1985 *The Future Impact of Automation on Workers.* Oxford: Oxford University Press.

Lilja, J. 1984 "Läkemedelskontrollen: ett mångtydigt begrepp." *Svensk Farmaceutisk Tidskrift* 88:26-31.

--------- 1984 "The Nationalization of the Swedish Pharmacies." Department of Social Pharmacy, Uppsala University. Typescript.

Lindblom, C. E. 1977 *Politics and Markets.* New York: Basic Books.

McGinn, R. E. 1978 "What is Technology?" In P.T. Durbin (1978).

Majone, G. 1986 "Government by Discussion: The Role of Policy Analysis in Democratic Policymaking." In *The Power of Public Ideas,* ed. R. B. Reich. Cambridge, Mass.: Ballinger.

de Man, R. 1987 *Energy Forecasting and the Organization of the Policy Process.* Ph.D. diss., University of Amsterdam.

Margolis, J. 1978 "Culture and Technology." In Durbin (1978).

Martino, J. P. 1972 *Technological Forecasting for Decision-making.* New York: Elsevier.

Merton, R. 1976 *Sociological Ambivalence.* New York: Free Press.

Merton, R. 1957 *Social Theory and Social Structure* Glencoe, Ill.: Free Press.

Meyer-Abich, K. 1984 *Wege zum Frieden mit der Natur.* Munich: Hanser.

Meyer-Abich, K. and R. Ueberhorst (eds) 1985 *Ausgebrutet--Argumente zur Brutreaktorpolitik.* Basel, Boston, and Stuttgart: Birkhäuser.

Mitcham, Carl 1978 "Types of Technology." In Durbin (1978).

Naess, A. *Democracy, Ideology and Objectivity.* Oxford and Oslo: Universitetsforlaget.

Nurmi, H. 1984 "Social Choice Theory and Democracy: A Comparison of Two Recent Views." *European Journal of Political Research* 12:325-33.

Offe, C. 1983 "Legitimation Problems in Nuclear Conflict." Paper Presented at the Somso Meeting on the Nuclear Energy Debate, Utrecht, Netherlands, June 24.

Perrow, C. 1979 *Complex Organizations.* 2nd ed. Glenview, Illinois: Scott, Foresman. (First ed., 1972).

Platt, J. 1969 "What We Must Do." *Science,* p. 1115.

Reichenbach, H. 1982 *Modern Philosophy of Science.* New York: Greenwood.

Rorty, R. 1985 "Habermas and Lyotard on Postmodernity." In Bernsten (1985b), 161-175.

Rosenberg, N. 1982 *Inside the Black Box: Technology and Economics.* Cambridge: Cambridge University Press.

Schadewaldt, W. 1979 "The Concepts of Nature and Technique According to the Greeks." In Durbin (1978).

Schon, D.R. 1969 "Managing Technological Innovation." *Harvard Business Review* 47:156-172.

Scott, P. B. 1985 *The Robotics Revolution: The Complete Guide for Managers and Engineers.* Oxford: Basil Blackwell.

Seaborg, G. T. 1973 "Science, Technology, and Development: A New World Outlook." *Science.*

Shaiken, H. 1985 *Work Transformed: Automation and Labor in the Computer Age.* New York: Holt Reinhart Winston.

Simon, H. A. 1977 *Models of Discovery and Other Topics in the Methods of Science.* Dordrecht, Holland: Reidel

Sinai, I. R. 1978 *The Decadence of the Modern World.* Cambridge, Mass.: Schenkman.

Sonnedecker, G. et al. 1974 *History of Pharmacy.* Madison, Wisc.: American Institute of the History of Pharmacy.

Stern, P. 1987 "Talking about Risk in an Atmosphere of Conflict." Typescript.

Ueberhorst, R. 1986 "Technologiepolitik -- was wäre das? Uber Dissense und Meinungsstreit als Noch-nicht-Instrumente der sozialen Kontrolle der Gentechnik." In Kollek, Tappeser, and Altner (1986).

-------------- 1985a "Zur Politikstilkrise der Kernerenergiediskussion." In *Kämpfer ohne Pathos: Festschrift fur Hans Matthöfer,* ed. H. Schmidt and W. Hesselbach. Bonn: Bund.

-------------- 1985b "Positionelle und diskursive Politik -- Die Bewährung einer demokratischen Technologiepolitik an den Chancen kritischer Argumente zur Brutertechnik." In Meyer-Abich and Ueberhorst (1985).

Ueberhorst, R. et al. 1983 *Planungsstudie zur Gestaltung von Pruf- und Burgerbeteiligungsprozessen im Zusammenhang mit nuklearen Grossprojekten am Beispiel der Wiederaufarbeitungstechnologie.* Wiesbaden: Im Auftrag der Hessischen Landesregierung.

Weber, M. 1968 *Economy and Society.* New York: Bedminister Press.

Weingart, P. 1984 "The Structure of Technological Change: Reflections on a Sociological Analysis of Technology." In Laudan (1984).

Weinstein, P. A. 1983 "Strategies for Public Policy in Labor Market Adjustment." Paper presented at Conference, The Impact of High Technology on Labor, May 24, George Mason University, Fairfax, Va..

Wellmer, A. 1985 "Reason, Utopia and the Dialectic of Enlightenment." In Bernstein (1985b), 35-66.

Wildavsky, A. and R. Tannenbaum 1981 *The Politics of Mistrust: Estimating American Gas and Oil Resources.* Beverly Hills, Calif: Sage.

Willer, D. and B. Andersson 1981 *Networks, Exchange and Coercion.* New York: Elsevier.

Winner, L. 1983 "Technologies as Forms of Life." In *Epistemology, Methodology and the Social Sciences,* ed. R.S. Cohen and M.W. Wartofsky. Dordrecht, Netherlands: Reidel.

Wittrock, B. 1986 "Socal Knowledge and Public Policy: Eight Models of Interaction." In *Social Science and Governmental Institutions,* ed. C. Weiss and H. Wollman. London: Sage.

-------------- 1984 "Useful Science and Scientific Openess: Baconian Vision or Faustian Bargain." In *Science as a Commodity,* ed. M. Gibbons and B. Wittrock. Essex, England: Longman.

INDEX

ABOUT THE AUTHORS

Tom R. Burns is Professor of Sociology at The University of Uppsala, Sweden, and Clarence J. Robinson Professor at George Mason University, Virginia. He is also program co-director, Social Science Theory and Methodology Program, the Swedish Collegium for Advanced Studies in the Social Sciences. Among his publications are *The Shaping of Social Organization: Social Rule System Theory with Applications* (1987); *The Shaping of Socio-economic Systems* (1986); *Technological Development with Reference to Hydro-power, Nuclear, and Alternative Energy Technologies* (1985); *Man, Decisions, Society* (1985); *Work and Power* (1979).

Reinhard Ueberhorst has been a member of the German Parliament and the West Berlin Parliament. He served as chairman of the German Parliamentary Commission on Future Nuclear Energy Policy. At present he is a member of the Parliamentary Commission of Enquiry, "Technology Assessment" and is a member of the Social Democratic Party's Commission on Basic Values. He writes on current issues and runs a policy consulting office in Germany. Ueberhorst has edited *Municipal Environmental Policy* (1983, in German) and *Devolution-Arguments Concerning Fast-breeder-reactor Policy* (1985, in German). His numerous articles include "Technology Policy—What Was That" (1986), "Normative Discourse and Technological Development" (1984), and "Progress-Technology-Humanity" (1980).